HOLIDAYS AND HIGH SOCIETY

HOLIDAYS AND HIGH SOCIETY

THE GOLDEN AGE OF TRAVEL

LUCINDA GOSLING

IN ASSOCIATION WITH
MARY EVANS PICTURE LIBRARY

The
History
Press

First published 2019

The History Press
The Mill, Brimscombe Port
Stroud, Gloucestershire, GL5 2QG
www.thehistorypress.co.uk

British Library Cataloguing in Publication Data.
A catalogue record for this book is available from the British
Library.

ISBN 978 0 7509 9008 0

Typesetting and origination by The History Press
Printed in Turkey by Imak

CONTENTS

"FAMOUS TRAINS and THEIR DESTINATIONS"

A feature of the "Railway Ball" at the Royal Opera House, Covent Garden, to be given in aid of the Kensington, Fulham and Chelsea General Hospital on December 11, will be a pageant entitled "Famous Trains." Some of these "trains" are reproduced on this page

Mrs. A. G. McCorquodale, producer and designer of the pageant, as "St. Moritz"

The Hon. Mrs. John Russell depicting "The Blue Train"

A back view of Miss Betty Hulton featuring "Cannes"

Photographs by Sasha

Lady Lindsay-Hogg typifying "The Engadine Express"

Princess George Imeritinsky, obviously "The Golden Arrow"

INTRODUCTION

DURING THE INTER-WAR YEARS, if there was ever an excuse to dress up in costume, the members of British high society took it. Pageants, fundraising balls, matinees and themed galas demanded that well-known ladies of the day dress up in spangled gowns and vertiginous headdresses, and pose obligingly for press photographers. These events usually had a charitable function, and raised money for worthy causes, but they were also an opportunity for rising stars of the social scene and more established 'well-knowns' to further their celebrity status.

In 1930, the Royal Opera House played host to the Railway Ball in aid of the Kensington, Chelsea and Fulham Hospital Fund. Among the costumed groups was one entitled 'Famous Trains and their Destinations', and illustrated weekly magazine *The Bystander* published five of the socialites in their outfits. Betty Hulton, daughter of the newspaper proprietor Edward Hulton, dressed in a gloriously flamboyant beach pyjamas suit and enormous hat, represented the smart French Riviera resort of Cannes. Mrs John Russell came as The Blue Train – the luxury express that whisked passengers from Paris to the Côte d'Azur overnight. Then there was Lady Lindsay-Hogg as the Engadine Express, bound for the smart Swiss ski resorts, and Princess George Imeretinsky as the Golden Arrow. Finally, the organiser and producer, Mrs Alexander McCorquodale, better known as the novelist Barbara Cartland, was resplendent as St Moritz, with a pine tree balanced precariously on her head. These fabled trains and high-class resorts would have been familiar not only to those who attended the Railway Ball, but also to most of *The Bystander*'s readers. Whether you had the means or not to holiday on the Riviera or ski at St Moritz, these names were all recognisable, signifying a glamorous and cosmopolitan world populated by a social elite.

The railway revolution of the nineteenth century had in turn triggered a tourism revolution in its wake. As working-class day-trippers flooded into rapidly developing British seaside resorts such as Blackpool, Scarborough and Margate, the upper classes set their sights on something and somewhere more exclusive, more refined, more picturesque and usually much further away. They looked towards Europe and North Africa and began to colonise and carve out

◀ Page from *The Bystander*, 3 December 1930, featuring society women wearing their costumes for the Railway Ball to be held at the Royal Opera House on 11 December that year. Taking part in the 'Famous Trains' pageant were Miss Betty Hulton as Cannes; Mrs A.G. McCorquodale (novelist Barbara Cartland), producer and designer of the pageant, as St Moritz; Mrs John Russell as The Blue Train; Lady Lindsay-Hogg as the Engadine Express; and Princess George Imeretinsky as the Golden Arrow. (© Illustrated London News/Mary Evans)

places where they could mingle with like-minded people. They expected hotels offering every conceivable home comfort; where the entertainment was cherry-picked from the best of Paris cabaret and London's West End; and where the sporting facilities were unrivalled.

Many resorts germinated as a result of the Victorian obsessive belief that poor health could always be cured by a spell spent in a milder climate. Consumptive patients flocked to spas in Germany, sanatoriums in Switzerland and the sun-soaked towns of the French Riviera, but over time, and with the added impetus of royal or aristocratic patronage, places that had begun as health resorts expanded and transformed into playgrounds for the idle rich.

Just as the travel-themed costumes of the Railway Ball were deemed of interest to *The Bystander*'s readers, so the real-life holiday resorts, and the people who stayed there, became newsworthy. Along with similar magazines such as *The Tatler* and *The Illustrated Sporting and Dramatic News*, *The Bystander* fed its readers a lively mix of news covering fashion, theatre, society, sport, politics, society gossip, motoring and travel. They published photographs of celebrities, whether actors, sporting figures, politicians or aristocrats, on the beach, dressed in the latest fashions, sipping cocktails at a poolside bar or looking chic on the golf links at Le Touquet. They were doing things most mere mortals might only ever dream of, but then, as now, mere mortals wanted to read about it.

Browsing through these contemporary periodicals, many of the same faces emerge at different resorts; some socialites seemed to do little else other than travel from one to another. Actress Gladys Cooper is pictured at both Frinton-on-Sea and the Venice Lido; Lady Diana Cooper seemed to prefer the Lido too, but stars such as tennis champion Suzanne Lenglen, cabaret act the Dolly Sisters and the ubiquitous Duke of Westminster crop up on the Riviera, at Biarritz and Deauville with impressive frequency.

The Bystander, more disposed to concentrating on travel writing, would run 'winter sports' supplements and even published a Riviera Number each year, its staff decamping to the French coast with the generous aim of providing their readership with pictures and prose that were based on first-hand experiences. Illustrations, cartoons and dazzling cover art by some of the finest illustrators of the day paid homage to these relatively far-flung places, while travel posters designed by some of the best artists of the genre, and fetching high prices at auction today, only added to their legendary status.

This book brings together eight of the most high-profile destinations favoured by high society during the last quarter of the nineteenth century and the first

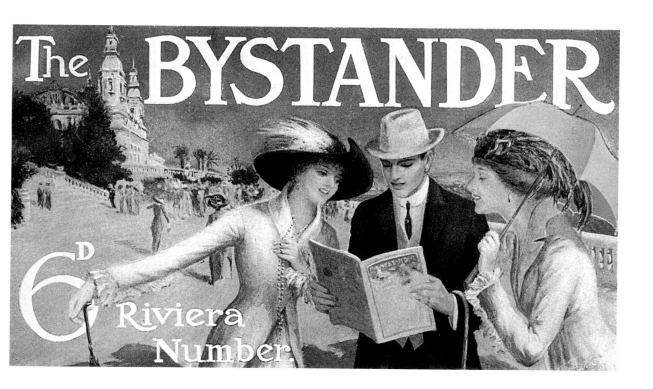

quarter of the twentieth. It is not an exhaustive list of high society's holiday habits, but it draws on the eclectic archives of the Mary Evans Picture Library, including contemporary magazines, brochures, posters, photographs and ephemera, to build a picture of the most celebrated resorts and the stories behind their success.

A century or more since the heyday of these resorts some, such as St Moritz, retain their expensive and exclusive allure, while others, like the smart riverside clubs and roadhouses in Britain that once teemed with Bright Young Things during the 1930s, have virtually disappeared. 'A Golden Age' often feels a hackneyed expression for defining an era, and yet for those with the wealth and leisure to enjoy the very best the world had to offer, that is exactly what it was. Travel posters of the inter-war years often urged people to 'Follow the Swallows' – a slogan that accurately summed up the seasonal migration of high society, and its tendency to flit from one resort to another. While the rich, famous and privileged followed those swallows, this book in turn invites us to follow them on their journey.

SUMMER ON THE FRENCH RIVIERA
BY THE BLUE TRAIN

PRINTED IN FRANCE

THE FRENCH RIVIERA

PLAYGROUND OF THE IDLE RICH

IN NOVEMBER 1922, *The Bystander* magazine opened its special Riviera Number with the following announcement:

> Well, here we are at the end of our pilgrimage, preparing to edit a real Riviera Number of The Bystander from the Hotel Carlton in Cannes. The blinds are drawn in Tallis Street, and we have left London to take care of itself. We have been received by the Mayor, the Mediterranean is whispering a welcome through the open window, and the sun is shining all the more brightly on our account.

The magazine's residency at one of the smartest hotels in the most elegant resort on the French Riviera was significant enough to attract the attention of the *New York Herald*. For the benefit of its American readers, the newspaper reported that only the previous January the Carlton had been the headquarters of the international peace conference. Now it was being colonised by 'the London illustrated weekly, *The Bystander*, and artists, humorists, poets, photographers, fashion and gossip-writers will be transferred for a week from London to Cannes.'

As journalistic jobs go, it didn't get much better.

The Bystander had launched in 1903 as a sibling to the more grown-up weekly illustrated paper *The Graphic*, and from the beginning, each Wednesday, delivered a lively mix of sport, political satire, news from stage and society,

◀ 'Summer on the French Riviera by the Blue Train'. (1928, Charles-Jean 'Alo' Hallo, L. Serre & C. Imp., Paris, 66 x 101cm, Collection Alessandro Bellenda)

ÉLÉGANCE
ART
BEAUTY

MONTE CARLO

SPORT
SUN

HAVAS

fashion, gossip, motoring and travel. The French Riviera, combining as it did several of these themes in one seductive stretch of French coastline, was of particular interest and the magazine began to produce its annual Riviera Number before the First World War. It was published in November to coincide with the annual migration of the British upper classes to sunnier climes, when the London season, Cowes Week and grouse shooting in the North were over and the encroaching British winter made a Mediterranean break, if not quite essential, then certainly enticing.

Four years later, *The Bystander* chose the Majestic Hotel in Nice as its base and one of its contributors, the comic writer Reginald Arkell, posed the question, 'Will the Riviera Remain?' Bearing in mind that *The Bystander* staff no doubt enjoyed their annual excursion, it was a rhetorical question but Arkell quoted Arnold Bennett to prove his point that the Riviera's charms were long lasting and universally appealing:

> Amid all the implacable competition of holiday resorts the Riviera more than maintains its prestige ... The serpentine string of pearls continues to glitter more and more brightly. And you continue to go south. The Mediterranean has been the home of pleasure for centuries simply because of its natural advantages. When you have variegated and sublime scenery, equable winter temperature, cataracts of sunshine and a sea that is bluer than any artist can paint it, you have all the raw material and much of the finished material, of an unsurpassable winter pleasure resort.

A decade on, Charles Graves, a journalist and author of several popular books on the Riviera, was also waxing lyrical in *The Bystander*, conjuring a destination of pure perfection with his words:

> Bathing in transparent, warm, blue sea, slicing your drive round an olive plantation, eating ripe figs off the branches, playing lawn tennis in the shade of eucalyptus trees, drinking bronxes made with tangerine juice instead of the synthetic product of bottled oranges – these are joys reserved for visitors to the Riviera.

◄ Elegant, art deco style advertisement for Monte Carlo designed by A. Harfort and published in *The Bystander*, December 1931. (© Illustrated London News/Mary Evans)

Composed of around 140 miles of coast stretching from Hyères, just east of Marseilles to Menton on the French–Italian border, the Riviera's beginnings as a tourist destination are generally attributed to one man: the Scottish novelist

◄ Guests at the Summer
Sporting Club at Monte
Carlo Beach enjoy the
novelty of gambling in
the open air. Illustration
by Fortunino Matania
in *The Bystander*,
17 July 1934.
(© Illustrated London
News/Mary Evans)

▶ On a speedboat near the Summer Sporting Club, Monte Carlo, the Hon. Kay Norton (right), Mrs Richard Hoffman of New York (left) and Lady Castlerosse (foreground). Katherine Norton, the youngest daughter of Lord Grantley, was a dress designer and frequently declared one of the best-dressed women in Britain. Doris Delevigne, Lady Castlerosse, the socialite wife of gossip columnist Valentine Browne, Viscount Castlerosse, was a habitué of the Riviera and other fashionable resorts. Her string of affairs, both before and during her marriage, were well known, but the society magazines kept discreetly quiet on the matter, instead preferring to concentrate on Lady Castlerosse's neat figure and chic sense of style. She died of an overdose of sleeping pills aged just 42. (© Illustrated London News/Mary Evans)

▶ Sun worshippers at Juan-les-Pins have suncream 'tattoos' painted on to their backs. The tanning craze was a dominant feature of Riviera life during the inter-war years. A 'Miss Suntan' beauty pageant was even held at the Belle Plage, Cannes, from 1929. Imagno/Mary Evans)

LE SOLEIL TOUTE L'ANNÉE
PLM
ROGER
BRODERS
SUR LA CÔTE D'AZUR
PRINTED IN FRANCE

Tobias Smollett. Smollett travelled to that section of the French coast in the eighteenth century and the letters he wrote during his two years in Nice were published in 1766 as a book, *Travels in France & Italy*, in which he frequently referred to the glorious weather and the faultless scenery. The interest triggered by Smollett's descriptions is reflected by huge sales of a contemporary phrase book for travellers: *A Manual of Conversation in Six Languages, English, German, French, Italian, Spanish and Russian*. In the mid eighteenth century, the journey from England to the South of France took a gruelling sixteen days by boat, horse-drawn coach and river-ferry crossings. Fraught with potential hazards and discomforts, the phrase book contained dialogue for every eventuality along the way, from 'I should like to take my harp and portmanteau by the stagecoach' to the rather alarming 'Disengage the horseman from under the coach'.

The next significant figure to champion the Riviera was Henry Peter Brougham, Lord Brougham and Vaux, former Lord Chancellor. Having retired from a political career, Brougham travelled with his daughter to southern Europe in 1834, en route to Rome via Genoa. But the outbreak of cholera in Marseilles meant that he was unable to pass a quarantine border into Nice, and was forced to break his journey and stay in the small fishing village of Cannes – a settlement with a population of around 300 at the time. Cannes was a world away from England, or 'fog-land' as Brougham dismissively labelled his native country, and he felt compelled to stay, building a villa in the Italianate style and using his influence to persuade the French Government to create an artificial harbour. He even imported grass so as to create a traditional English lawn around his house.

Brougham died in Cannes in 1868, but his pivotal role in the resort's development is commemorated by a statue that stands today, looking out over the harbour. Just a decade after his death, Cannes had grown at an incredible rate with almost fifty hotels, numerous villas and imported plants – mimosa, acacia, eucalyptus and palm trees – which, though not native, would forever after be associated with the Riviera landscape. The English built their own churches and soon the Cercle Nautique yacht club, founded by the Duke of Vallombrosa in 1864, was to become one of the most exclusive destinations on the Riviera. Membership cost 100 guineas, which would buy access to seventeen bedrooms, a luxurious bar, a smoking room and a long gallery with stage, all run by footmen in powdered wigs and knee breeches serving caviar and smoked salmon from eleven in the morning.

◄ 'Le soleil toute l'année sur la Côte d'Azur'. (1930, Roger Broders, Lucien Serre, Paris, 63.3 x 100cm, Collection Alessandro Bellenda)

◄ Millionaire's paradise. A view of Eden Roc at Cap d'Antibes in 1932; the bathing and sunbathing complex was fashioned out of the rocky coastal outcrop and was where smart society came to see and be seen lounging on the famous orange mattresses. (© Illustrated London News/Mary Evans)

Nice was also growing rapidly, particularly after 1860 when Napoleon III agreed to provide Italy with financial and military aid in exchange for the city, which came back under French rule. Roads were built and the railway was extended from Marseilles to reach Nice in 1864 – improvements that were to result in an unprecedented influx of '*hivernants*' – winter visitors. Between 1861 and 1874, the number of people from overseas residing in Nice rose from just under 8,000 to 25,000 – an astonishingly rapid increase. The economy of the French Riviera, which previously derived a modest income from olive oil, flowers and other forms of agriculture, was transformed into a rumbling service industry dominated by an annually swelling cycle of tourism. When French poet Stéphen Liégeard published his ode to the Riviera in 1887 and entitled it 'La Côte d'Azur', the area gained a brand name steeped in lyrical romance. But its status as a winter destination for Northern Europeans remained fixed until after the First World War.

The third major settlement on the Riviera, Monte Carlo, owed its success to a French casino owner named François Blanc. Blanc already ran a casino in Bad Homburg and sensed an opportunity in Monte Carlo, when he bid for and won a fifty-year franchise to run the casino. Blanc engaged Charles Garnier, architect of the Paris L'Opéra, to build a squat confection of a casino – at a time when gambling was banned in many parts of Europe. Wanting to create a resort dedicated not just to gambling, but also to pleasure and luxury, Blanc also built grand hotels, laid out gardens and introduced gas and electricity. When the Prince of Wales, the future King Edward VII, visited Monte Carlo in 1875, its success was guaranteed. Kings and dukes came to play at Monte Carlo's tables, but by the standards of its more polite neighbours, its reputation would always be racy and rascally.

Menton, a few miles east of Monte Carlo, had established itself as a health resort for invalids – mainly consumptives. It was pretty, unspoilt and unpretentious, with plenty of quiet walks and vistas to be enjoyed by visitors, though lacked the sophisticated thrills of Monte Carlo. *The Traveller* magazine in a report of 1900 admitted that the proximity of Menton's 'naughty neighbour, only twenty minutes by train … is considered by a goodly number as a great addition to Menton's many attractions'. For those who did take the train to 'Monte' for an evening's entertainment, maids would usually travel ahead of them with clothes to change into on arrival, so avoiding the indignity of entering the casino or opera in a travel-crumpled gown.

◄ An open-air manicure at Juan-les-Pins in 1928. (© Illustrated London News/Mary Evans)

However, some writers were less inclined to acknowledge Monte Carlo's attractions. Gordon Home, writing in *Along the Rivieras of France & Italy* in 1908, described the casino as:

a group of showy exhibition buildings. No writer has yet failed to pour contempt on the flamboyant rococoesque style of architecture of the headquarters of the gambling world; and one feels no inclination to say a word in its favour, saving that it is, perhaps, quite in keeping with the lack of self-respect generally exhibited by the habitués of Monte Carlo ...

Pickpockets, loudly-dressed women of many nationalities, and men representing the depraved element in the moneyed classes of all the countries of Europe, turn Monte Carlo into a spot which cannot fail to be repugnant.

He went on to describe dark consequences of the town's *raison d'être*. Monte Carlo's authorities were apparently careful to cover up any suicides as a result of a run of bad luck – such things weren't good for business. Home even recounted the grisly rumour that the police kept bodies until the end of the season after which they discreetly disposed of them by dropping them in weighted cases into the sea.

It is no surprise that Queen Victoria, who first visited the Riviera in 1882, preferred the more genteel bolt-holes of Menton, Hyères, Grasse and Nice's Anglo-Russian suburb, Cimiez. She made a day trip to Monte Carlo during that first holiday, but in her journal commented, perhaps with some preconceived prejudice, 'One saw very nasty disreputable looking people walking about at Monte Carlo ...' While her son and heir played *chemin-de-fer* and enjoyed the attentions of ladies of the demi-monde, the highlight of the elderly Queen's days was a sedate ride in a cart around well-manicured gardens, pulled by a donkey called Jacko.

Other members of the British royal family were frequent visitors to the Riviera. Prince Arthur, later the Duke of Connaught, bought the Villa 'Les Bruyéres' at Saint-Jean-Cap-Ferrat after the First World War in an area first 'discovered' by King Leopold II of the Belgians. It was wryly described by William Somerset Maugham as 'the escape hatch from Monaco for those burdened with taste'. His younger brother Prince Leopold, Duke of Albany, died in Cannes on 28 March 1884. Suffering what is now believed to be haemophilia and mild epilepsy, he had travelled to the Riviera on the advice of his doctor, and slipped on tiles at the

◀ Three evening outfits by Drecoll, Premet and Paul Poiret, for the arrival of the *Flying Cloud* at Cannes, by an unattributed artist in *Art-Goût-Beauté*, April 1924. *Flying Cloud*, one of the era's most luxurious yachts, belonged to Hugh Grosvenor, 2nd Duke of Westminster, otherwise known as 'Bendor'; only the most exquisite couture would suffice for an evening on board. From the mid 1920s to the mid 1930s, the Duke had an affair with Coco Chanel. He gave her a parcel of land at Roquebrune-Cap-Martin, where she built her villa, La Pausa. (Mary Evans Picture Library)

Cercle Nautique Yacht Club. The minor accident led to his death at the age of just 30. His daughter, Princess Alice, Countess of Athlone, later became the owner of the Villa Nevada, where her father had died.

After the British came the Russians, especially when the opening of the railway in 1864 witnessed the arrival of Tsar Alexander II in Nice, leading to a diaspora of Russian society and culture in the South of France. Among the prominent Russian influencers was Grand Duke Michael of Russia. Something of a maverick within the Romanov family, he had been banished from court due to his morganatic marriage. But in Cannes he was patron and head of society, where he established the Mandelieu Golf Club and dabbled in a number of building and development projects. In Nice, the St Nicholas Orthodox Cathedral was funded by Tsar Nicholas II and consecrated in 1912. Its continuing status as Western Europe's largest Eastern Orthodox church is a lasting reminder of Russia's firm foothold in the area.

The prominent British contingent on the Riviera was well chronicled in *The Traveller* magazine, which kept readers up to date with all the latest hotel openings and improvements to the area. In its weekly column 'Sunday Morning Notes', it frequently described the various Anglican churches established in the Riviera towns and the clerical personalities presiding over their flocks. It described the Memorial Church of St George at Cannes as 'the church par excellence of continental Anglicanism'. In another issue, it drew attention to the arrival of a Mr W.J. Lancaster – a graduate in history from Worcester College, Oxford, whose arrival on the Riviera would be a great relief for English families seeking tutors for their sons. In *The Bystander*, advertisements for John Taylor Estate Agents in Cannes and Nice demonstrated just how embedded the British were. Queen Victoria died in 1901, sighing wistfully on her deathbed, 'Oh, if only I were at Nice, I should recover.' *The Traveller* noted how the mourning for the late Queen was just as keenly observed in the South of France as it might be in Mayfair.

The British had been the pioneers of Riviera travel and the Russians had joined them in colonising the area, but it was the Americans who helped mould the area into a holiday destination in tune with the modern era in the years following the First World War. Numerous hotels were requisitioned as hospitals during the conflict, with some American soldiers finding themselves recuperating under the Mediterranean sun. Word spread. 'More and more big liners come from America to Monaco each year,' observed *The Chicago Tribune* in 1922, musing in 1926 if the area's popularity with Americans was due to Prohibition.

◄ English film actress Betty Balfour playing the banjo at Juan-les-Pins. Photograph by Raoul Barba, *The Tatler*, 15 August 1928. (© Illustrated London News/Mary Evans)

◀ Mrs Frank Jay Gould (right) (1893–1985), née Florence de Caze, wife of wealthy philanthropist and businessman Frank Jay Gould. Together with him, she patronised the arts and helped to develop areas of the French Riviera including Juan-les-Pins. Bronzed, with a megawatt smile, she was renowned for getting up early to play sport regardless of how late she had gone to bed the previous night. Pictured with French tennis superstar Suzanne Lenglen at Monte Carlo in 1934. During her dominance of women's tennis in the 1920s, Lenglen repeatedly won tournaments at Cannes, Nice, Monte Carlo, Biarritz, Le Touquet, Deauville and Pourville. (© Illustrated London News/Mary Evans)

◀ Noël Coward working on his tan at Eden Roc in the 1920s. (Imagno/ Mary Evans)

One American had already wielded considerable influence on the Riviera. The newspaper magnate James Gordon Bennett ran the *Paris Herald* (later to become the *International Herald Tribune*) from his home in Beaulieu, and consistently showered praise on the Riviera from the 1880s, claiming, for one thing, that its sunshine was superior to anywhere else. He also published daily lists of eminent visitors to the area, helping to create the cult of the Riviera celebrity.

By the 1920s, Americans were arriving in increasing numbers, bringing with them money, but also new habits and a less formal way of doing things. One of these was sunbathing – a novel leisure activity that was to become a defining feature of the Côte d'Azur. It was Coco Chanel who first made the tan fashionable when she stepped off the Duke of Westminster's yacht at Cannes in 1923 with gleaming brown skin. Where Chanel led, others followed and the suntan as a statement of health, wealth and style was adopted and popularised by the Americans and a younger generation of British socialites. The phenomenon also led to the French Riviera transitioning from an exclusively winter resort to a summer sun destination. Until then, visitors had stuck to a fairly rigid timetable, arriving from November each year, but departing before Easter. William Scott, in his 1908 volume on the Riviera, confirmed these migratory habits:

> As sure as Easter has come and gone, whether it be early or late, whether the season be early or the reverse, so surely do most of the strangers – especially the English – think it absolutely necessary to leave the Riviera; though most of them would be puzzled to give an intelligent reason for the move.

The two people generally accepted in Riviera histories as responsible for this quiet revolution are Gerald and Sara Murphy – a wealthy American couple who escaped from America in the early 1920s in search of a freer existence. After spending time in the bohemian atmosphere of Paris, from there they migrated south to the Riviera on the recommendation of Gerald's friend and Harvard contemporary Cole Porter. Porter didn't return to the Riviera, lured instead by the Venice Lido, but the Murphys stayed. They found the sandy, seaweed-choked beach of La Garoupe at Antibes and, while they built a home, to be called Villa America, they stayed in the largely vacant Hôtel Cap d'Antibes during the summer. Between 1925 and 1929, they lived an idyllic existence, entertaining friends including F. Scott Fitzgerald and his wife Zelda, Ernest Hemingway and Pablo Picasso, playing treasure hunts with their children, swimming, sunbathing,

painting and treating guests to good food and company, all arranged with a simple but memorable elegance. The impression the Murphys and their lifestyle made on Fitzgerald, moved him to immortalise them as the characters Dick and Nicole Driver in his final novel, *Tender is the Night*. The book's dedication is to 'Gerald and Sara: many fêtes'.

'The Riviera has been described as the playground of the idle rich, but is also the workshop of famous people', wrote *The Sketch* in 1926, reflecting on the influx of not only wealth and breeding, but of talent and creativity. H.G. Wells bought a villa at Grasse, Edith Wharton was a regular visitor to the Riviera and set a portion of her novel, *The House of Mirth*, there. In 1927, she purchased a villa, Sainte-Catherine du Castel, in the hills above Hyères, where she created a superb tropical garden, which is now a public park. Katherine Mansfield, suffering from chronic tuberculosis, spent some of the happiest months of her short life at the Isola Bella in Menton, and W.B. Yeats died in Cannes. They, along with other ailing writers such as Robert Louis Stevenson and D.H. Lawrence, chased the hope that the Riviera had mythical properties of renewal. For a while it did. Katherine Mansfield died in a sanatorium near Fontainebleau, but had written in her journal just days before her death: 'I simply pine for the South of France.' Like Queen Victoria two decades earlier, the health-reviving benefits of the Riviera loomed large in the imaginations of those who had experienced it.

William Somerset Maugham lived on the Riviera for four decades from 1926 at the Villa Mauresque on Cap Ferrat. He once famously quipped that the Rivera was 'a sunny place for shady people' – a quote so perfectly phrased it has been an epitaph from which the region will probably never quite escape. Maugham's own escape from England, and marriage, allowed him to co-habit with his lover, Gerald Haxton – an American eighteen years his junior – in the more permissive atmosphere of southern France. In a feature on Maugham at home in *The Sphere* in 1954, Haxton was coyly referred to as his 'secretary-companion'. The couple also lived in some style, employing thirteen servants before the Second World War, though the novelist admitted, 'It is easy to be idle on the Riviera', finding his work ethic constantly hampered by the daily round of tennis, bridge and cocktail parties.

Elsewhere, other significant figures in the arts found a welcoming and conducive environment to work. The pioneering Ballets Russes performed each summer in Monte Carlo, and Rex Ingram, the film actor, director and producer, worked from the Victorine studios just outside of Nice. The area's association with film would be further established with the founding of the Cannes Film

◄ The beach at Juan-les-Pins, by Helen McKie, *The Bystander*, November 1929. By the end of the 1920s, the resort had become one of the most fashionable on the Riviera, aided by the building of the imposing, art deco Hôtel Provençal (background) by Frank Jay Gould. (© Illustrated London News/Mary Evans)

NICE

LES NOUVELLES AFFICHES CAPPIELLO
DEVAMBEZ Gravᵗ Imᵖᵉ
52, Rue Beaujon PARIS

Cappiello
1927

EDITION DU SYNDICAT D'INITIATIVE

Festival in 1939; Cannes had paid a considerable sum to be chosen over Biarritz as the location for a festival that would rival Venice. Planned to open on 1 September, the first festival was abandoned due to the outbreak of the Second World War, re-establishing itself in 1946. It remains a leading highlight of the film industry calendar today.

The dancers Isadora Duncan and Margaret Morris both separately established schools on the Riviera, and corralled their pupils into striking artistic poses on rocky beaches or in sun-dappled palm groves. Many other actors, writers and artists naturally gravitated to the Côte d'Azur, intent on finding their own piece of paradise, mixing with the nobility and the nouveau riche who had always made the coast their playground. The portraits in *Riviera Personalities*, published in 1925 by the *Monte Carlo & Menton News* and with a preface written by the popular novelist and Riviera resident Edward Philips Oppenheim, reflected the diversity of the area's celebrities. Tennis star Suzanne Lenglen rubs shoulders with Raoul Gunsburg, director of the opera at Monte Carlo; the novelist and playwright Baroness Orczy is featured alongside Georges Fleury, manager of the Hôtel de Paris in Monte Carlo.

The fictional Hôtel des Étrangers in Fitzgerald's *Tender is the Night* eventually became 'a summer resort of notable and fashionable people'. The real life Hôtel Cap d'Antibes, once a secret summer retreat for the Murphys and their circle, also began to capitalise on its success and styled itself as an exclusive haven for an elite clientele. A saltwater swimming pool and sun terraces were cut into the adjoining cliffs, while changing rooms constructed underneath the hotel's restaurant ran with hot and cold showers and came with such extras as a weighing machine. It was named Eden Roc. It was here that press photographers prowled to capture chic holidaymakers bronzing in the sun, or, as the papers wrote, 'getting a good sunburn' as they laid out on the Roc's famous orange mattresses.

Elsewhere, the small village of Juan-les-Pins, with its south-west-facing sandy beach, was also developed at an astonishing rate, largely due to the speculations of American millionaire Frank Jay Gould. Gould took over the small casino there and built the art deco La Provençal – a hulking ten-storey, 200-room hotel to accommodate enough guests to make his casino profitable. It worked. By the mid 1920s, Juan-les-Pins was one of the most glamorous destinations on the Riviera's coastline. Hotels were located close enough to the beach for guests to saunter down in their beachwear, and bob around in the warm, tideless sea. 'There are some strenuous damsels,' observed 'A Grass Widower', writing in

◄ With its flower markets, fragrance industry and the traditional 'Battle of the Flowers' carnivals in Nice and beyond, flowers were an enduring theme used to promote the region. (Nice, 1927, Leonetto Cappiello, Devambez, Paris, 80 x 118.4cm, Galleria L'IMAGE, Alassio)

the

BYSTANDER

1¹⁄₂

CASINO

MOTORING

DANCING

RACING

RIVIERA
NUMBER

HAFFENDEN

The Illustrated Sporting and Dramatic News in June 1925, 'who teach dancing and physical culture on the beach,' as well as some 'aquatic tricycles that are enormous fun'. But the emphasis was on swimming and 'acquiring that delicate nut-brown shade that is obtained by sun basking' – a daily pattern of activity that would have been unthinkable to the winter visitors of the belle époque era. For them, promenading along the Croisette in Cannes, or the Promenade des Anglais in Nice, had been the daily ritual, carrying a parasol to shield oneself from the midday sun. With today's knowledge of sun safety, the tanning obsession during the inter-war years, as described by Ferdinand Tuohy in *The Sphere* in 1938, had clearly reached alarming heights:

> The human steaks lie there, slightly comatose, all day long, save for meals and periodic entry into the tepid water. When they lay down book or paper to talk it is usually to discuss the body-curve or tan of others. Most of them are covered in oil and lotion skin-dyes. Not a few are bandaged or show carmine patches where the skin has come off from too precipitate work.

Aside from the cult of sun worshipping, there were plenty of other activities and entertainment to keep the most demanding visitor satisfied. Tennis tournaments attracted the era's leading players. When Suzanne Lenglen played Helen Wills Moody at the Carlton Club in Cannes, she showed typical Riviera sangfroid by turning up in her ermine coat and sipping champagne before winning the match. There were world-class golf courses – a necessity for any self-respecting high-class holiday resort – water-skiing, aqua-planing, tir aux pigeons (pigeon shooting) at Monte Carlo, cabaret shows and the native tradition of carnivals. The highlight of the latter was the spectacle of the Battle of the Flowers, where florally festooned cars and floats paraded through the streets of Nice and other towns in the region. In Villefranche, boats covered in flowers chugged through the harbour as passengers threw blooms at each other across the waves.

As other smaller towns began to grow through virtue of their beaches and sunbathing facilities, Monte Carlo, with its slightly jaded and tawdry reputation, engaged the services of American publicist and party-giver Elsa Maxwell, who had already applied her skills with some success to promoting the Venice Lido. Among the more crackpot ideas suggested by Maxwell was a tar and rubber beach, but she knew as well as anyone that 'King Soleil' was the new ruler on the Riviera, and advised that a new pavilion and summer casino were built, along with a 50-metre pool and tennis courts. Le Sporting opened in 1927.

◄ Impression of the Palais de la Méditerranée by Helen McKie, *The Bystander*, 5 February 1930. The new palatial casino was built at Nice in 1929 by American millionaire Frank Jay Gould, and its marble staircase, seen here, was the widest in the world. Shortly before its opening, Douglas W. Thorburn, wrote in *The Bystander*, 'An enormous sum of money has been spent in an endeavour to make this the most magnificent and most up-to-date casino in Europe and certainly I have never seen its equal, although the finishing touches have yet to be added.' (© Illustrated London News/Mary Evans)

Monte Carlo's successful rebrand continued into the 1930s with art deco style advertisements in the illustrated press embellished with seductive promises: a sun terrace for every room in the Monte Carlo Beach Hotel; the *plage dorée* (gilded beach), the Monaco Speed Grand Prix (from 1929) and an artistic season under the patronage of His Highness Prince Louis II of Monaco.

Meanwhile, in Nice, Frank Jay Gould opened the gargantuan Palais de la Méditerranée casino, with a marble staircase acknowledged to be the widest in the world and a restaurant with the capacity to seat 1,000 diners. Its modern mood was the perfect setting for his third wife Florence, one of the Riviera's most glamorous residents whose love of gambling and champagne was renowned. An expert in jet-skiing and water-planing, she founded the water-skiing club at Antibes and, no matter how late she went to bed, had a reputation for getting up bright and early ready to swim or play tennis. Frank died in 1956 but Florence lived until 1983, continuing to live life to the full. Her cocktail parties in the 1960s during the Cannes Film Festival were the stuff of legend.

Florence also took delight in fashion, being one of the first women on the Riviera to adopt the beach pyjama trend in the 1920s. For all the emphasis on the new spirit of casualness, clothes were a serious business on the Riviera. Margaret Bradley, writing in *The Sketch* in 1928, described the unofficial daily fashion show in Cannes: 'On the Croisette at about eleven the fashionable life begins. There are throngs of *flâneurs*, passing silhouettes at whom we would fain gaze longer to learn more intimately the secret of their chic.' She mentioned too how it was considered '*dernier cri*' to have your frock match your car – fashion on a shoestring was not an option for the serious Riviera *habitué*.

Throughout the 1920s, *The Bystander* saw fit to regularly run a column titled 'What Shall We Wear on the Riviera'. In 1925, Edith Boulter advised jumper frocks for day and evening gowns for after hours, singling out Jean Patou for 'simplicity of line and perfection of cut'. Patterned knitted jerseys were also popular during the 1920s, 'made by Russian refugees ... launched by Gabrielle Chanel ... a kind of glorified Fair Isle confection in softer colourings and more intricate patterns'. For beach pyjamas, the Russian designer Mary Nowitzky (Maria Novitskaya) created hand-painted silk ensembles specifically for the Riviera or Venice Lido. British-born Captain Edward Molyneux, who had branches of his couture house in Cannes and Monte Carlo as well as Paris, offered pastel-coloured tweed jumper suits, ideal for golf, and exquisite georgette evening gowns in plain colours. 'Nobody knows better than he just the right type of evening gown for the Riviera,' wrote Boulter. The previous year, she had reminded readers: 'as he

◄ Château l'Horizon: the extensive and luxurious villa built at Golfe Juan by American actress Maxine Elliott, who had been one of the great Edwardian beauties of the stage. The villa was designed by Barry Dierks and cost £80,000 when it was built in 1931. Among its outstanding features were shady balcony windows and a swimming pool with a chute out into the sea. Many famous figures stayed or were entertained at the villa over the years, including Winston Churchill and the Duke of Windsor. © Illustrated London News/Mary Evans)

F. ROMOLI
929
STAGIONE
GIVGNO
SETTEMBRE
ALASSIO
RIBASSI FERROVIARI
SERVIZI TURISTICI-AVIOLINEE
TUTTE LE ATTRATTIVE
INFORMAZIONI PRESSO:
ENTE AUTONOMO STAZIONE DI CURA
DIZIONI SUPERCARTELLO
35903 BARABINO & GRAEVE - GENOVA

has a large establishment in Cannes, those who hanker after his [Molyneux's] models will be able to buy them when they arrive without breaking the journey in Paris, which is likely to be almost as grey and cold as London during the summer months.' Molyneux was one of several top Parisian couturiers, including Jeanne Lanvin, Chanel and Jean Patou, who opened branches at the Riviera resorts, offering convenience to their well-heeled customers and further cementing the area's reputation as a centre of taste and style. In 1927, in direct response to the burgeoning tanning trend, Patou launched its first suntan oil, Huile de Chaldée. Chanel brought out Huile de Jasmin in the same year.

Edward Molyneux lived as well as worked on the Riviera, and his home, Villa Capponcina at Cap-d'Ail, was frequented by a stream of glamorous friends who were also customers – most notably Gertrude Lawrence, who was snapped on several occasions posing in the villa's gardens. In 1931, to inaugurate his newly built swimming pool, Molyneux threw a 'swimming dinner' where the dress code stipulated 'beach outfits'. The guest list was stellar, including Lord and Lady Louis Mountbatten, Noël Coward, Grand Duke Dmitri and his wife, Lady Juliet Duff, Lady Cynthia Mosley, Cecil Beaton and the era's leading style maven, Daisy Fellowes. Outshining the glitzy guests were a display of arc lights, fireworks and an American orchestra to provide the latest jazz tunes.

Another owner among the Riviera's 'villarchy' was the actress Maxine Elliott. Once one of the most successful Edwardian actresses on the London and New York stages, and a canny businesswoman, Maxine retired comfortably to the Riviera, to a luxurious hideaway designed by the region's most celebrated architect, Barry Dierks. At the Château l'Horizon, Maxine played hostess to a stream of A-list guests including Winston Churchill, Anthony Eden and the Duke and Duchess of Windsor. The Windsors lived close by at La Croë, where the Duchess created a luxurious sanctuary of impeccable taste with the help of interior decorators Sybil Colefax and Lady Mendl (Elsie de Wolf), and visitors were bemused to hear the incongruous skirl of a Scottish piper as they sat to dinner in the Antibes twilight. Maxine's villa had a private bridge across the railway line, each room was en suite with a shaded, sea-view balcony, a hatch served hot meals to sunbathing guests on the terrace and, for those brave enough, the sublime, blue-tiled pool had a chute that deposited swimmers straight into the Mediterranean. As The Bystander commented, practically the only individual without a title to stay at the villa was Maxine's pet monkey, Kiki, who, although locked in mutual adoration with her owner, had a tendency to terrorise guests by sitting in the changing rooms and stealing items of clothing.

◀ Leaving Menton and crossing the French–Italian border, the Italian Riviera towns were once colonised by a significant British ex-pat community, in particular the town of Alassio, which was admired by composer Edward Elgar and the writer and artist Edward Lear, among others. The Second World War was to lead to an exodus of the British, but this vibrant poster signifies that, in its heyday, Alassio could equal the French Riviera towns for sun and sophistication. Today, the town's English-language library remains as a curious relic of that dominant British presence. (Alassio, 1929, Filippo Romoli, Barabino & Graeve, Genova, 70 x 100cm, Galleria L'IMAGE, Alassio)

The novelist Baroness Orczy was another renowned hostess, holding regular salons at her villa, Le Bijou, at Monte Carlo. In 1922, *The Bystander* reported that she 'received over sixty friends at tea at her villa the other day'. Six years later, and there was no sign that her entertaining zeal had diminished: 'There was Baroness Orczy's reception, she herself always the most piquant and tactful of hostesses, eternally moving about, yet eternally by the side of the person who needs her presence, an artist at hospitality, an artist in the selection of her friends.'

◄ The Pullman Express boasted similar levels of luxury to The Blue Train and offered the opportunity of daytime travel. (Côte d'Azur Pullman Express, 1929, Pierre Fix-Masseau, Imp. L. Danel, Lille, 62 x 100.5cm, Collection Alessandro Bellenda)

Before long, The Blue Train was confirmed as an icon of popular culture. In 1924, the Ballets Russes performed a one-act ballet, *Le Train Bleu*, written by Jean Cocteau and with costumes designed by Chanel. Three years later, Lily Elsie starred in a light stage comedy, also called *The Blue Train* and written by Reginald Arkell and Don Titheridge, while Agatha Christie's Belgian detective, Hercule Poirot, was called upon to solve a murder there in her 1928 novel, *The Mystery of the Blue Train*. In London's Stratton Street, The Blue Train restaurant, now Langan's Brasserie, was opened by an Italian Savarini, who commissioned painter Geoffrey Houghton Brown to produce murals on the theme of travel. Meanwhile, in Paris, Le Train Bleu restaurant at the Gare de Lyon, where The Blue Train once departed, is a more grandiose affair with belle époque murals of Riviera scenes paying homage to the train's famous route.

Ensuring the journey was as pleasurable as arrival remained an important factor in the continuing popularity of resorts with wealthy visitors. The Côte d'Azur Pullman Express, operated by PLM, first ran in December 1929 and offered luxury to rival The Blue Train, with many decorations carried out in glass by Lalique. Whereas The Blue Train travelled through France at night, the Pullman Express offered a daytime service from Paris, where British travellers embarked having travelled via the Golden Arrow from London Victoria and Calais. Other routes endeavoured to offer the same levels of service and comfort, such as the Sud Express, which travelled to Biarritz and then over the border into Spain, or the Engadine Express, bound for Switzerland. The Orient Express from Paris to Cairo, introduced in 1928, reduced the previously arduous journey to Egypt to just one week.

► Leaving gloomy Paris and heading to sunnier climes. The Blue Train departing from Paris' Gare de Lyon. (The Blue Train departing from Paris Gare de Lyon station, 1986, Michel Lamarche (original gouache), 79.8 x 45cm, Collection Alessandro Bellenda)

▲ Côte d'Azur, PLM (Paris–Lyon–Méditerranée).
(1934, Munetsugu Satomi, Le Novateur, Paris,
61 x 99.2cm, Collection Alessandro Bellenda)

▲ 'La Côte d'Azur à une nuit de Paris'
(La Côte d'Azur à une nuit de Paris,
1926, Emile-André Schefer, Lucien
Serre & C., Paris, 76.7 x 106.5cm,
Galleria L'IMAGE, Alassio)

▲ In 1926, Southern Railways launched the all-first-class Golden Arrow train to whisk British travellers from London Victoria to Dover, where they would take a ferry across the Channel. At Calais, they would then take the Flèche d'Or, run by the Chemins de Fer du Nord to Paris, from where they would continue their journey via the Pullman Express. (La Flèche d'Or – Golden Arrow, 1926, William Spencer Bagdatopoulos, Sungravure Process (England), 65 x 101cm, Galleria L'IMAGE, Alassio)

▲ Côte d'Azur Pullman Express. A portion
of the original interiors from a Pullman
car of the Wagons-Lits Co. Interior design
by René Prou; original glass decoration
with the bacchanalian maidens by René
Lalique; moquette and carpet textiles by
Suzanne Lalique-Haviland. (Collection
Alessandro Bellenda)

▲ Londres–Vichy Pullman. (1927,
Jean-Raoul Naurac, Lucien Serre & C.
Imp., Paris, 78 x 107cm, Galleria L'IMAGE,
Alassio)

▲ The journey from London to Cairo took
seven days in 1930 via the luxurious
Orient Express. (Londres–Le Caire,
Simplon Orient Express, 1930, Jacques
Touchet, Lucien Serre & C. Imp., Paris,
61.5 x 100cm, Galleria L'IMAGE, Alassio)

PARIS-ORLEANS RAILWAY OF FRANCE AND WAGONS-LITS C°
TWO DE LUXE TRAINS
PYRENEES
CÔTE D'ARGENT
AND
SUD-EXPRESS
TO
BIARRITZ
THE PYRENEES
THE BASQUE COUNTRY
AND
SPAIN
COMFORT SPEED AND SMOOTHNESS
P.O._PUBLICITÉ N°7
IMP. CHAIX _ PARIS _ 1-28. (Encres Lorilleux)

◄ Biarritz Côte Basque.
1927, Dabo (Geoffroy
d'Aboville), Fredi Salzedo,
Biarritz, 76 x 104cm,
Galleria L'IMAGE,
Alassio)

► 'The Gay, Warm
South', by C. Morse,
The Bystander, 28
November 1928. Scene
in Biarritz at the height
of the winter season,
showing the Hôtel du
Palais in the distance.
Among the cosmopolitan
crowd is a gentleman in
hunting attire – a sign
of the hunt meetings
that were a popular
feature of Biarritz life.
© Illustrated London
News/Mary Evans)

► Bar Basque in 1934
- the rendezvous that
everyone' in Biarritz
frequented for an
aperitif, often at one of
the pavement tables.
© Illustrated London
News/Mary Evans)

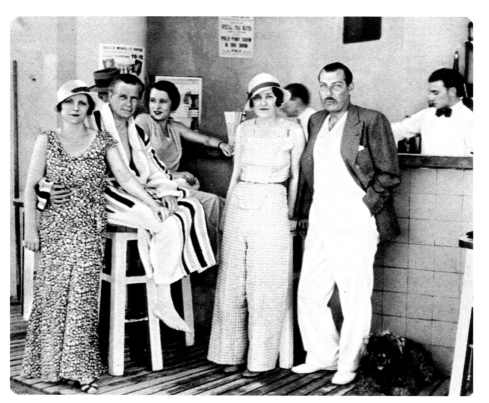

◄ A group of 'well-knowns' at the beach bar of the Chambre d'Amour at Biarritz in 1932. From left, Mr and Mrs Ormond Lawson-Johnston, who had hosted the Prince of Wales during his stay; Lady Furness (Thelma Furness, mistress of the Prince of Wales); Miss Leary; and the Marquis de Bermejillo. Two years later, Lady Furness would find herself usurped as royal mistress after she had introduced her friend Wallis Simpson to the Prince. (© Illustrated London News/ Mary Evans)

◄ Artist's impression of the bathing pool at the Chambre d'Amour, with its colonnades and sun loungers lining the pool. (© Illustrated London News/Mary Evans)

During the inter-war years, Biarritz was the destination typically selected by the smart set when temperatures on the Riviera became unbearable. Its position on the Atlantic coast meant that, while sunshine was in abundant supply (though not guaranteed), weather fronts kept the air fresh and the ocean, with its thunderous waves crashing against the rocks on Biarritz's shoreline, was invigorating. Sunbathing and swimming were the main draw on the sandy beaches, which were dotted with colourful beehive-shaped tents (the Plage Basque was considered the most fashionable), but there were plenty of other amusements unique to Biarritz. It boasted two fine golf courses, the Plateau du Phare and the Chiberta, which was distinct for employing girl caddies 'who stride around bravely, their close-fitting berets at a jaunty angle', reported *The Sphere* in 1929.

Berets, being the traditional headwear of the Basque region, were enthusiastically adopted by visitors to Biarritz during the 1920s and '30s, sported as an accessory to swimsuits or sundresses. The greatest beret-wearer of the period was local boy and leading tennis player Jean Borotra, nicknamed 'The Bounding Basque' due to the athleticism he displayed on court, all while wearing a beret. His style, and that of fellow Basque player Henri Cochet, was no doubt influenced by the Basque game of *pelota*, which required an energetic level of stretching and jumping.

Pelota was a novel spectator sport for British visitors to the area, but became a craze everyone was keen to take up after the Prince of Wales tried his hand at the game in 1931. Bullfighting in Bayonne or across the Spanish border at San Sebastián was another form of entertainment for some, although many Brits found the spectacle appalling. *The Bystander* reported on meeting the actress Virginia Cherrill outside the stadium one day, clearly distressed at what she had just witnessed and also struggling to find her car. Undaunted, the magazine then continued to segue smoothly into describing her linen skirt suit in a shade of butter yellow! From one blood sport to another, British visitors may have been rightly squeamish about bullfighting, but they were quite happy to partake in the hunting available at Biarritz: a weekly meet was held throughout the winter season.

Like all resorts, Biarritz had a casino – two in fact. The Bellevue, with its peach and cream decor, was more intimate than the behemoths of Monte Carlo and Nice. Such was the informality that one newlywed couple, Mr and Mrs Coats, who visited in 1922, were so engrossed in a game of *chemin-de-fer* that Mrs Coats brought a sandwich to the gaming table 'and munched whilst calling

BIARRITZ

out "Banquo!"' Nights at the casino included dances, cabaret and music at its nightclub, Chez Ambrose, named after the famous band leader Bert Ambrose, who was imported from London for the summer season and was able to indulge his own dangerous gambling habit while there.

Elsewhere, Biarritz society congregated at several popular rendezvous. Most famous was Bar Basque, part of the Grand Hotel, where it was a daily ritual to sit around the tables spilling from the pavement on to the street to enjoy an aperitif. Sonny's Bar, at the back of the Carlton Hotel, was a fashionable rival to Bar Basque, while other venues, such as the Café de Paris, Dinali's and Casanova's, ensured Biarritz nightlife never became stale.

Biarritz could also boast a branch of Bricktop's – an offshoot of the famous Parisian bistro, run by the African American singer and entertainer Ada Smith, the eponymous Bricktop. Her friends and acquaintances included Cole Porter, F. Scott Fitzgerald and the Aga Khan, to whom she once famously taught the Charleston. In Paris, Bricktop's was the place to be, but sketch artist Pamela Murray's account of one evening at the Biarritz branch implies it was just as lively:

We went on to Bricktop's – la boite run by a red-headed negress of personality. Lady Furness was there, in scarlet as usual [Thelma Furness, a girlfriend of the Prince of Wales]. Mme Dubonnet's pearls were only outshone by her emeralds, with Mrs Edward Barron's diamond ring a runner-up … We were given a bottle of champagne each for supper, so do you wonder if I noticed nothing more?

◄ Illustration by Roger Brard from the September 1929 issue of French fashion magazine Art-Goût-Beauté, suggesting an outfit suitable for Biarritz. The brightly coloured scarf rippling in the bracing Biarritz breeze forms a picturesque outline, while the elegant borzoi dog – one of the most fashionable breeds of the period – completes the chic ensemble. (Mary Evans Picture Library)

Such nights might be discussed the following morning at the Chiberta clubhouse. Biarritz was renowned for its golf and Chiberta was one of its two excellent courses, its exclusivity clear by the number of Rolls-Royces parked outside. The clubhouse was, according to *The Bystander* in 1926, 'where everybody meets everybody and hears the latest gossip of how so-and-so made half a million francs last night, and where the latest beauty buys her complexion'.

No doubt people were discussing Madame Dubonnet and her dazzling jewels. The former Jean Nash had married Paul Dubonnet, one of the four heirs to the Dubonnet drinks empire, after he had divorced his wife Christane Coty, who herself had come from the wealthy family behind one of France's biggest fragrance houses. Their marriage had set tongues wagging, not least because of the Dubonnet family's fury that Paul had failed to arrange a pre-nuptial agreement prior to saying 'I do'. Regularly acknowledged as one of the

GONE BASQUE! SOCIETY BOMBACHO-ED, BÉRET-ED, AND PELOTA-CRAZY.

Sporting visitors to Biarritz have gone crazy over pelota, the Basque ball game, ever since the Prince of Wales tried his hand at it. And, not content with that, some of the smartest have gone completely Basque as to clothes, bursting out into the entire outfit—béret, bombachos (trousers), and espadrilles, and carrying the national walking-stick known as a makhila.

SPECIALLY DRAWN AT BIARRITZ BY BRYAN DE GRINEAU.

◄ 'Amusements in Biarritz', by Bryan de Grineau (1883–1957), *The Sketch*, 30 September 1931. Holidaymakers trying out the Basque sport of *pelota*, wearing a beret of course, while sunbathing is de rigueur and a costume ball keeps things interesting. (© Illustrated London News/Mary Evans)

► Cover of *The Sketch* featuring Mrs Gerard d'Erlanger, formerly the pianist Edythe Baker, posing prettily for photographers underneath a parasol at Biarritz in 1932. Born in poverty in Kansas, Edythe's talent as a boogie-woogie pianist saw her find fame in America and England in the 1920s. Her musical career came to an end upon her marriage into the wealthy d'Erlanger family. (© Illustrated London News/ Mary Evans)

The Sketch

No. 2068. — Vol. CLIX.   WEDNESDAY, SEPTEMBER 14, 1932.   ONE SHILLING.

A BLONDE IN BRONZING BIARRITZ : MRS. GERARD D'ERLANGER.

Mrs. Gerard d'Erlanger is one of the host of well-known English visitors to spend a basking holiday in the South of France. The huge striped umbrella and big hat make a charming setting for her fair loveliness. Mrs. d'Erlanger was, before her marriage, the "star" pianiste, Miss Edythe Baker. Her husband is one of the sons of Baron d'Erlanger.

◄ Madame Paul Dubonnet, formerly Mrs Jean Nash and regularly declared the best-dressed woman in Europe, on the Miramar beach at Biarritz in 1932 while her husband, of the drinks dynasty, sunbathes nearby. It was gossiped that Jean's faultless style had been acquired through the wallets of her four previous husbands, and Paul's decision to marry her had caused a family rift. Nevertheless, the couple's relationship endured. (© Illustrated London News/Mary Evans)

'world's best-dressed women', Mme Dubonnet's passion for fashion had been financed by her previous four wealthy husbands. The Dubonnets had reason to be concerned but, in fact, the marriage was a success.

The other daytime social hub was the romantically named Chambre d'Amour by the beach: a large swimming pool with a cascading waterfall at one end and a high diving board at the other, a bar, a colonnade of pseudo-classical columns and a row of *cabanes* lining one side of the pool. These tended to be inhabited by the Biarritz elite. Among these was the American Ginnie O'Malley Keyes, wife of Lieutenant Colonel Middleton O'Malley Keyes, who lived most of the year in Biarritz at their villa, Castel Meretmont; an invite to one of her Sunday luncheon parties was keenly sought. She had a brood of grown-up children, the eldest of whom, Hamilton 'Ham' O'Malley Keyes, married Lady Iris Mountbatten, a great-granddaughter of Queen Victoria, in 1941. Besides the numerous O'Malley Keyes were Mr and Mrs Ormond Lawson-Johnston, hosts to the Prince of Wales when he visited Biarritz in 1932, and the elegant Marques and Marquess Portago. The Marques, born into Spanish nobility, was a prominent polo player and a noted dandy. '"Tony" Portago changes his clothes a great many times in the course of the day, and they are all new', remarked Pamela Murray in her *Sketch* column. It is difficult to gauge whether she was impressed or not. Mr and Mrs Claude Leigh were also habitués of the Chambre d'Amour, or the 'Chamber of Horrors' as Claude glibly put it (when not on holiday, he ran a property company specialising in social housing; his remark was not without some architectural expertise). His wife was one of Biarritz's most stylish women, although, being blonde and fair-skinned, she eschewed sunbathing.

Another visitor to the Chambre d'Amour was the Prince of Wales, who would often appear before lunch for a swim. Unfortunately, it was also a favourite haunt of press photographers who roamed around the poolside and bar, taking photographs of socialites who were usually happy to pose for them. The Prince was a prize subject, of course, but his desire for privacy led one particularly persistent photographer to be forcibly removed one morning during the Prince's 1932 holiday. Despite this hiccup, the Prince liked Biarritz. He liked the society, he liked wearing the rakish berets and he very much liked the golf. He played obsessively, either with the professional golfer Archie Compston or the secretary of the Chiberta club, Major John Hind. In 1933, it was reported in *The Sketch* that the Prince of Wales was golfing as usual and having a 'really quiet holiday; but will probably go to more parties if Prince George turns up'.

◀ Elegant spectators at the polo ground at Beyris, halfway between Biarritz and Bayonne, which was opened in 1923 by the King of Spain. The polo season at Biarritz started in August and continued until the middle of September or, at the latest, mid October. Illustration by Edmund Blampied, *The Bystander*, 10 September 1924. (© Estate of Edmund Blampied/ILN/ Mary Evans)

St JEAN DE-LUZ

ROB MALLET-STEVENS

"Succès"

H. CHACHOIN Imp. Paris. 1928

◄ Situated halfway
between Biarritz and
the Spanish border,
St-Jean-de-Luz first
gained popularity with
the English during the
Peninsula War, when
Wellington took up
winter quarters in 1813
at Château St Anne, and
later, No. 2 rue Mazarin.
With its bay of fine
sand, the resort grew
in the early decades of
the twentieth century
to include several
hotels (including Hôtel
d'Angleterre, complete
with an English Club in
its annexe), the Casino
de la Pergola and the
Nivelle golf course.
St-Jean-de-Luz, 1928,
Rob Mallet-Stevens,
L20 x 158.7cm,
H. Chachoin Imp. Paris,
Collection Alessandro
Bellenda)

The Prince of Wales' younger brother was a reliable plus-one at any party; urbane, sophisticated, keen on cocaine and happy to flirt with both women and men, he would settle down before his elder sibling, marrying Princess Marina of Greece in November 1934.

However, in August of 1934, *The Sketch* gave a brief mention to another visitor to the Chambre d'Amour. 'Mrs Wallace [*sic*] Simpson looking very pretty with her dark hair parted in the middle', it reported, offering no further information and leaving the reader to work out who Mrs 'Wallace' Simpson was. What was not mentioned was that Mrs Simpson had been personally invited to Biarritz, as a member of the Prince of Wales' party. It was a sign of a deepening relationship that two years later would lead him, as King Edward VIII, to abdicate the throne in order to marry her. Biarritz had played its small part in yet another royal romance, but this one would have seismic consequences. The Prince of Wales' grandfather, King Edward VII, had used his holidays to Biarritz to discreetly and conveniently compartmentalise his relationships with other women. His grandson had instead developed an obsession that would shake the monarchy to its core. A monument to Edward VII, unveiled by Lord Hardinge in 1922, commemorates the King's link with the resort. 'If the Prince Regent made Brighton,' declared more than one magazine columnist, 'then King Edward VII made Biarritz'.

3

DEAUVILLE AND THE NORTHERN FRENCH COAST

PARIS BY THE SEA

THE COUNTRYSIDE AROUND DEAUVILLE on the coast of northern France is horse country. Racecourses, training establishments, stud farms and breeding stables have peppered the region since the area began to devote itself to the 'sport of kings' in the middle of the nineteenth century. Of the eight racecourses, the most prestigious is Deauville-La Touques, laid out in 1860 at the behest of the Duc de Morny, half-brother of Emperor Napoleon III and a racing connoisseur. Morny planned to make the racecourse the central attraction of a new, modern resort – the first of France's *plages à la mode*. It was named Deauville.

Deauville was a town manufactured purely for pleasure. Its neighbour Trouville, just across the River Touques, had already grown from a fishing village into a modest resort. But Morny had more ambitious plans for the site that would become Deauville. Formerly nothing more than sand dunes with a scattering of cottages housing barely more than 100 peasants, Morny's Deauville took just a few years to rise from the sands. It included a port, elegant villas, a tree-planting programme, a hotel and, to attract the wealthiest visitors and satisfy his own devotion to the sport, a racecourse. The arrival of a railway station, as with all burgeoning holiday resorts, provided the finishing touch.

A 1912 poster by the French caricaturist 'Sem' (Georges Goursat, 1863–1934) commissioned to promote the opening of the casino. Sem also produced an annual each year caricaturing the resort's visitors. Among the famous faces here are Polaire, dancer and courtesan Émilienne d'Alençon, painters Giovanni Boldini and Paul César Helleu, and Raoul Gunsbourg, director of the Monte Carlo opera house, all enjoying a convivial bathe in Deauville's waters. Deauville, 1912, 'Sem' Georges Goursat, Etabl. Minot, Paris, 74 x 104cm, Galleria L'IMAGE, Alassio)

151 DEAUVILLE - PLAGE FLEURIE
La Potinière

◄ 'Le Five o' Clock at Deauville', by Edmund Blampied, *The Bystander*, 21 July 1926. An impression of the polo ground at Deauville during the tea hour. The magazine informed the reader that afternoon tea, 'that formerly despised meal', has become fashionable again among *l'haut monde* on the Continent. Jersey-born Blampied (1886–1966) was a frequent contributor to *The Bystander* magazine of elegant watercolours featuring the glamorous and privileged classes at fashionable resorts around Europe. (© Estate of Edmund Blampied/ILN/Mary Evans)

◄ A view of the bustling La Potinière Café at the Plage Fleurie, Deauville, in the early 1920s, where Deauvillites congregated for a pot of shrimps and an aperitif. (Jazz Age Club Collection/Mary Evans)

Early visitors to Deauville enjoyed a genteel and sedate holiday experience, shared among the social elite who could afford to gather there. Gentlemen would go riding in the morning, leaving ladies to attend to the morning toilettes or go down to the beach for a 'foot bath', which was little more than a paddle. Bathing itself was something of a rigmarole, involving the necessary use of bathing huts and attendants, with their ropes providing a literal lifeline to nervous swimmers. Villa luncheon parties might then take up several hours, fuelled by champagne and coffee. Afterwards, Deauville society would gather at the racecourse. A similar timetable would be repeated the following day.

The collapse of the Second Empire in 1870 saw a temporary reversal of Deauville's fortunes, but around the turn of the twentieth century, when Trouville's mayor, M. Latellier, was voted out of the town, he simply shifted across to perform his civic duty in Deauville. He engaged a former waiter from Maxim's, Eugene Cornuche, as his '*animateur*' – a resort manager responsible for arranging and conducting a variety of amusements that would elevate Deauville beyond any rival resorts. Knowing part of Deauville's charm lay in its compact size, Cornuche chose not to subject the town to the urban sprawl suffered by some Riviera settlements. Instead he ensured a concentration of round-the-clock amusements guaranteed to satisfy a demanding and highly sophisticated audience who became known as 'Deauvillites'. For good measure, the resort's beach was re-christened '*la plage fleurie*'.

Deauville's stock was once again on the rise. In the years leading up to the First World War, Cornuche engaged some of the world's greatest artistes to bolster its reputation. 1912 was considered a brilliant season, with performances from the great Nijinsky and the whole town succumbing to the latest dance craze, the tango, transforming Deauville into Tangoville for a time. Sem (George Goursat), France's most famous cartoonist, started his first Deauville album this year – something he continued to produce annually until his death in 1935. He was also commissioned to design a poster advertising the opening of the casino that season, which he designed with caricatures of France's most well-known personalities, including Polaire, Émilienne d'Alençon, Giovanni Boldini, Paul César Helleu and Raoul Gunsbourg all enjoying a convivial bathe in Deauville's waters.

Until the end of the First World War, the bulk of Deauville's visitors were French, but in the early 1920s, the resort began to attract a British and American contingent. With the London season over by August, society migrated in their droves from the capital, and where better than Deauville, just three and a half hours from Paris or a short flight from Croydon airport? The Deauville season

▲ Racing, gambling, polo, tennis, cocktails, yachting and bathing: Deauville's delights encapsulated in one picture by caricaturist Tony Wysard for *The Bystander*, 16 August 1939. Wysard has peppered his illustration with a number of Deauville's notable visitors. The bespectacled Aga Khan is at the casino in the foreground of the picture; the Duke of Westminster in yachting attire squints through a telescope; and in the distance is Winston Churchill emerging from the sea, ubiquitous cigar in mouth. (© Illustrated London News/ Mary Evans)

PLAYTIME AT POURVILLE: ON THE PLAGE OF THE GRAND HOTEL

Visitors to Pourville, the delightful holiday resort on the Normandy coast near Dieppe, can never complain that there is nothing to do: for whether one's inclination is to bathe in the fine pool seen there or in the English Channel near by, to woo Dame Fortune at the tables in the Casino of the Grand Hotel, to play golf on the fine Dieppe links, to indulge in tennis on the Hotel courts, to play polo, to visit the races or to tread a measure in the ballroom, the opportunity is there at hand. Pourville is reached from London via Dieppe in a few hours.

▲ '"A Jewel of a Little Place". Playtime at Pourville, on the Plage of the Grand Hotel', by
Houghton, *The Bystander*, 24 June 1931. (© Illustrated London News/Mary Evans)

◀ Advertisement for Le Touquet in *Men Only* magazine, 1939. The fact that it was 'patronised pre-eminently by English people' was considered a selling point. (© John Frost Newspapers/ Mary Evans)

peaked during the three or four days leading up to the Grand Prix race held on the last Sunday of August, when hotels were full and the street cafés a lively ferment of gossip and cigarette smoke.

Ferdinand Tuohy, who reported on the goings-on of society at Deauville during the 1920s, described a typical day during this halcyon period. He would rise late and go for a swim, just before 'the peacock parade on the board-walk'. The boardwalk – or the Planches – was a long, wooden promenade built as a pathway over the sand. Not only did it allow ladies in heels to walk with ease, it also provided a readymade catwalk for Deauville's fashionistas.

Along with Cannes and Biarritz, Deauville was another of France's coastal centres of fashion, with a reputation for being terribly chic. Deauville was where Chanel chose to open her second boutique; Jeanne Lanvin and Jean Patou also had outposts here, the latter's clean-cut knitwear and androgynous styling feeling particularly at home. Photographers like the Seeberger brothers regularly haunted the Planches ready to take snaps of passing *modes*, and in so doing, established the first form of street-fashion photography. Likewise, fashion designers were savvy enough to realise the influence these photographs had when they were published in the press and made sure to send models in their latest designs to the Deauville races, where department-store buyers would be on the look out for the latest creations. The Boardwalk encouraged a contrived opportunity to achieve some celebrity. In 1926, *The Bystander* noted how young women in flamboyant bathing costumes of 'every colour of the rainbow' carried coloured balloons with them, 'adding an exquisite note of movement, light and colour to a slim figure wrapped in some gorgeous shawl of jazz-patterned wrap'. These were the Instagram moments of their day, and Deauville, with its beach runway and exclusive boutiques housed in immaculate fairy-tale-style half-timbered Norman buildings, was the place to be seen.

After his swim, Tuohy would visit La Potinière for a pot of shrimps and an aperitif – a habit made fashionable by the visiting King Alfonso XIII of Spain. If he felt more substantial victuals were required, then Ciro's, offering 'caviar, saddle of lamb, salad, champagne and all the trimmings' would satisfy any hunger pangs. The rest of the afternoon was spent either at his hotel or a bar whiling away the hours until 9 p.m. – the hour when Deauville's nightlife sprang into action. The next five or six hours would be spent dining, 11 p.m. being the favoured hour for dinner, dancing, gambling and enjoying cabaret. People would drift from Brummel's bar to Tardet's, run by the Basque Marquis d'Arhémp. Among the most popular was the bar run by celebrity boxer Georges Carpentier

◄ The former 1930 'Deb of the Year' Miss Margaret Whigham pictured with her husband, the American golfer Charles Sweeny, at Le Touquet, in *The Tatler*, 31 July 1933. Before her marriage, she had visited Baden-Baden, St Moritz and Cairo with her parents. Now, as the celebrated Mrs Sweeny, she was accompanying her husband on the annual Buck's Club golf expedition to the French resort, which was renowned for its golf. The press delighted in featuring photographs of her in a variety of chic outfits. (© Illustrated London News/ Mary Evans)

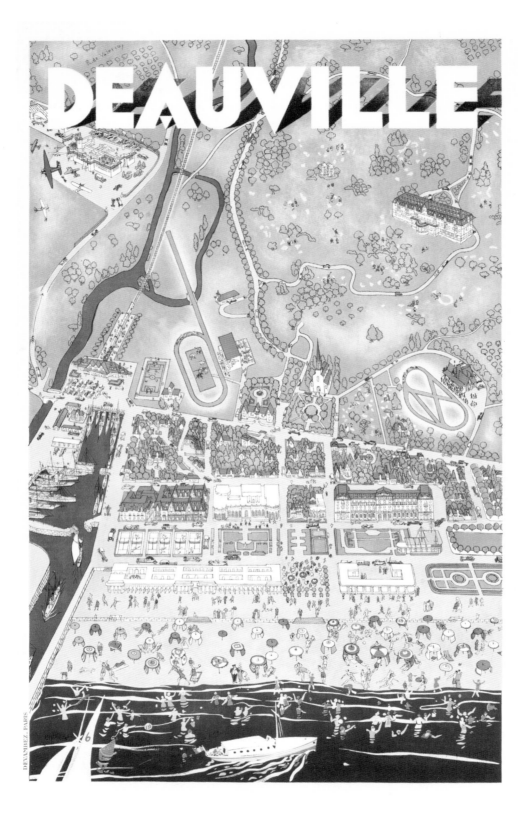

at the yacht club. As the sun rose, revellers would find breakfast, take a bath and finally fall into bed. This hedonistic existence took some stamina. Tuohy recalled the Comte de Ganay once remarking that, after three weeks in Deauville, he was going back to Paris 'to recuperate'.

Cornuche's formula for success was very simple. He believed in giving 'something definite, and preferably expensive to do every single moment of the day or night. I pick out a circle of very rich people and then go and plant myself in the middle of them!'

The regulars at Deauville did indeed include some of the wealthiest pleasure-seekers in the world. Racehorse owners Solly Joel and the Aga Khan were familiar faces; as was Gordon Selfridge, founder of the London department store, Bendor, Duke of Westminster, and André Citroën, scion of the motor manufacturing empire who once lost 9 million francs in one night at the Salle Privée. The Aga Khan's son, Prince Aly Khan, might be spotted at the Ambassadeurs restaurant as well as the celebrated Dolly Sisters, dressed in matching Jean Patou, and usually playing (and losing) huge amounts of Gordon Selfridge's money at the casino. Tuohy also mentioned Deauville's infamous 'Alimony Sisterhood' – a group of divorcees, mainly American, whose failed nuptials had left them wealthy enough to sit in the bars and restaurants of Deauville exchanging gossip about their various ex-husbands.

Before Cornuche died in 1926, he appointed a successor to carry on his good work and to uphold Deauville's reputation. François André, whose previous career had included working for an undertaker, controlled all aspects of Deauville, once declaring to Barbara Cartland that, 'Nothing is good that isn't expensive'. He built a theatre, knowing that providing alternative entertainment for the wives of some of the casino's most valued patrons would keep everybody happy. He also had the foresight to set up a crèche known as the Ducks Club, 'where small children can be parked off the Boardwalk, surrounded by all the trappings to amuse while their mothers are free to go and "play the horses" or to gamble in the casino'.

Another attraction, built while Cornuche was still alive and dedicated to the swimming and sunbathing brigade, kept Deauville ahead of any competitors. The Pompeiian Baths – a Greco-Roman fantasy of cool, marble colonnades and blue and gold, mosaic-covered walls – was situated right on the Grande Plage. Bathers stepped out of the 'ordinary' changing rooms into a courtyard carpeted with neat grass, while those who took the deluxe cabins emerged onto a flower-decked patio. 'Neither variety,' advised *The Sketch* magazine, covering this new

◄ An aerial view of the resort which was kept intentionally compact by its '*animateur*', Eugene Cornuché, who developed the town into a fashionable destination in the early 1900s. British visitors to the French north coast increasingly began to arrive via plane in the 1920s and this view may have been enjoyed by aviators approaching in their own aircraft. On 21 July 1930, a German Juncker monoplane crashed over Meopham in Kent on the way back to Croydon from Le Touquet. All passengers were killed including The Marquess of Dufferin and Ava, Viscountess Ednam, the daughter of the Duchess of Sutherland. The pilot, Geoffrey Rodd, had formerly set up a flying school in Brooklands and once smuggled Mary Cunningham-Reid's dachshund back from Deaville so her beloved pet might not spend months in quarantine. (Deauville, 1935 ca., Roger de Valério, Devambez, Paris, 60.2 x 96.5cm, Galleria L'IMAGE, Alassio)

BRVNELLESCHI

TROUVILLE

AFFICHES "LA MARTINELLA" MILAN
PARIS - Faubourg St. Honoré, 6

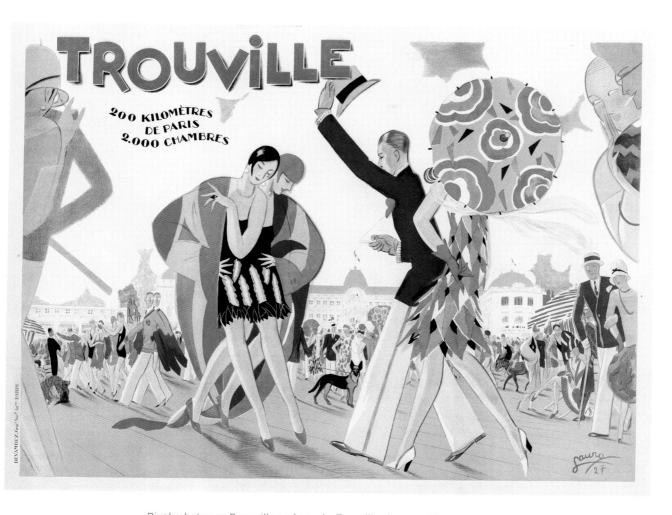

Rivalry between Deauville and nearby Trouville simmered for
decades and, although Deauville may have been considered
the pre-eminent resort on the northern French coast, Trouville,
as evidenced by these stunning posters designed by Umberto
Brunelleschi and Maurice Lauro, was determined to present itself
as a chic alternative to its neighbour.
(◄ Trouville, 1925 ca., Umberto Brunelleschi, Affiches La
Martinella, Milano, 70 x 100cm, Collection Alessandro Bellenda;
▲Trouville, 1927, Maurice Lauro, Devambez, Paris, 156.3 x 117cm,
Collection Alessandro Bellenda)

innovation, 'is advised for economical people.' At the baths' centre was an atrium, where a fountain splashed in a circular pool. A full-colour illustration of the baths by *The Sphere*'s leading artist, Fortunino Matania, conveyed to readers a sybaritic atmosphere of imperial Rome, and with it, the full extent of Deauville's capacity for luxurious escapism.

Deauville may have been the queen of the northern French coast, but for travellers seeking variety, there were other pleasant resorts to choose from, all vying to win a number of its wealthy customers. All sought to add their own special something to the tried and trusted formula of good beaches, casinos, nightlife and sporting facilities. In Mabel Howard's fashion column in *The Sketch*, 1929, she discussed how 'Deauville has reigned for so long as the ultra-smart plage for August', but went on to list a number of up-and-coming resorts such as Cabourg nearby and La Baule and Sables d'Or in Brittany, where 'daily gatherings of smart beach costumes' and 'a gay kaleidoscope of casino frocks at night' were becoming de rigueur.

Deauville's nearby neighbour Trouville was dubbed 'Paris-sur-mer' during the Edwardian era: a place catering to those with motor cars or yachts, and charging prices in proportion to their wallets. But as Deauville's star ascended under Cornuche's guiding hand, Trouville began to be outshone. 'The conquest of Trouville has been completed, and Deauville now reigns supreme,' declared *The Bystander* in 1913, '– so supremely that Trouville, save for one or two hotels and a few villas, can scarcely be said to exist. Its downfall is one of the most amazing events in the history of French holiday-resorts.' Fifteen years later, the rivalry rumbled on: 'Deauville built itself up on the experience of the older town; and Trouville wishes to goodness it wouldn't come butting in like that.' People did, of course, still go to Trouville and its belle époque casino, and it remains a thriving resort today. But the cream of society had shifted allegiance, and Trouville began to be quietly ignored by journalists and magazine editors.

Pourville, a few miles from Dieppe, was described by *The Bystander* as a 'jewel of a little place'. Significant development of the former fishing village during the inter-war years included the opening of the Grand Hotel, built in order to attract some of Deauville's customers. Designed in a style complementary to Pourville's charming architecture, the addition of an artificial village green in the town, surrounded by thatched cottages housing shops, only added to its mildly twee charm. During hot weather, hotel guests at the Grand were provided with sleeping porches that were covered with climbing roses and hung silver drapes, creating a magical fairy-tale ambience.

◄ Josephine Baker (1906–75) – American-born French cabaret artist, entertainer, activist and French Resistance agent – with her pet cheetah Chiquita at Deauville in 1930. Deauville's boardwalk on the beach provided the ideal photo opportunity for celebrities – especially a megastar like Baker. Chiquita had originally been given to her by a club owner to be used in one of her acts, but became a much-loved pet, accompanying her as she travelled and even sleeping in her bed. (© Illustrated London News/Mary Evans)

Le Touquet, situated on the Pas-de-Calais coast, was a comparatively modern resort, which is reflected in the number of stylish villas and public buildings, designed by local architect Louis Queteret, that still form stopping points for architectural tours of the town today. The land on which it was built was bought and developed by two British investors in 1902, and the town received official status a decade later. Its biggest draw was the golf course, argued by many to be among the world's best, and the casino, which was situated in a clearing in the pine forests that were planted during the nineteenth century. It famously became the Duchess of Westminster's hospital for wounded British soldiers during the First World War (No. 1 Red Cross Hospital) and its saloons, still hung with their immense chandeliers, were filled with hospital beds.

In 1936 Le Touquet opened its own aerodrome – a move that was to seal its popularity with the sporty, upper-class British. 'More and more Le Touquet is becoming an aerial suburb of London, to be treated as a week-end resort,' reported *The Bystander* in 1935, 'From Fridays to Mondays it is crowded to the roof, and the wagering at the roulette tables is so heavy that there is quite a boring interval between throws.' Advertisements targeted the British visitor with a promise that Le Touquet was 'The English-speaking resort'. P.G. Wodehouse, who owned a villa at Le Touquet, often played golf, as did the Prince of Wales, who was said to prefer the course to any other in Europe – and he had sampled most. Another frequent visitor was the golfer Charles Sweeny often accompanied by his stylishly turned out wife, the former Miss Margaret Whigham. The toast of London society, Margaret's 1933 wedding to Charles had been one of the news stories of the year and drew a crowd of thousands to the Brompton Oratory in Knightsbridge. Mrs Sweeny's husband did not approve of women playing golf, so she instead obligingly posed around the course, wearing something chic and sporty. The couple divorced amicably in 1945.

Le Touquet suffered badly during the Second World War. It was believed to be the most mined town in France and, in the aftermath, thousands had to be cleared from its beach. Damaged hotels were renovated and Le Touquet was eventually restored as one of Europe's leading sporting holiday resorts.

◀ Style on the beach.
Catwalk show at
Deauville, August 1935.
(Imagno/Mary Evans)

EXCELSIOR PALACE HOTEL

LIDO (VENEZIA)

4

THE VENICE LIDO

THE LURE OF THE LIDO

IN AUGUST 1926, 22-year-old Cecil Beaton arrived in Venice. Having left Cambridge without a degree the previous autumn, he had spent twelve months working, with reluctance and inefficiency, at the office of a friend of his father's in the City. He endured the job because his employer, Mr Schmiegelow, was tolerant, and in between tasks, he was able to spend time taking his portfolio to publishers or retouching photographs. But he struggled daily with the knowledge that his failure to find real employment was trying the patience of his father, and that his ambitions to have his photographs and designs printed in the press were continuously dashed by a stream of rejection letters. The news that the Baroness D'Erlanger, one of Venice's leading hostesses, was to hold a lavish costume ball had convinced Beaton that a trip to Italy could hold the key to the success he so desperately craved. A door had been opened by an invitation from two journalists, suggesting he accompany them – Alison Settle of *Eve* magazine and Mrs Whish of the *Daily Express*. Here was an event that brought together some of the most glamorous and influential members of society, in one of Europe's most fashionable, romantic and cosmopolitan settings. Not only did the idea appeal to Beaton's love of theatricality, but such an opportunity brought him within touching distance of the inner sanctum of smart society where, he felt certain, he could achieve success if given the chance. Determined to get there by whatever means necessary, he asked several friends if they could loan him the money before eventually persuading his father to give him the £20 needed

Fancy-dress balls and pageants were an integral part of the society holiday experience and nowhere more so than in Venice, with its historic tradition of carnival and masques. This art deco cover of a brochure for the Excelsior Palace Hotel references the typical eighteenth-century costume styles favoured by Venetians. (Jazz Age Club Collection/ Mary Evans)

to fund the trip, promising him, 'I really think I might be able to get something out of it.'

As a 'hanger-on', Beaton's experience of the costume ball, held at the Fenice Theatre, did not live up to expectations. A professional photographer was already in place and when he politely asked the Baroness' daughter, Princesse Jean de Faucigny-Lucinge (the former Baba d'Erlanger), if he could take her picture, she proved an uncooperative sitter. On another day, he managed to engineer a meeting with the great impresario Serge Diaghilev, the mastermind behind the Ballets Russes, who politely looked through all Beaton's costume designs and photographs, but gave no indication of offering him work.

Although the trip had not fulfilled any career ambitions, Beaton was captivated by Venice, and particularly by the Lido. Arriving on the short steamboat trip from the city, he marvelled at the vastness and vulgarity of the hulking Excelsior Palace Hotel, declaring it 'hideous' in his diary, 'but good fun'. In the hotel's lounge, he witnessed women sitting around in 'the most expensive pyjamas (with designs of dragons and birds of prey hand-painted in brilliant, sickening colours) and no shoes'. He noted with interest that many men also wore pyjamas – a flouting of convention that would have appealed to his flamboyant streak. And when he arrived at the beach to sunbathe and wallow in the warm waters of the Adriatic, he was dismayed to find his striped 'maillot'-style costume was inappropriate since most male bathers wore brief shorts. He resolved to acquire a pair as soon as possible. 'Venice is the place!' he wrote with a flourish at the end of his first day experiencing the delights of the Lido.

A narrow sand bank of around 10 miles, facing the mouth of Venice's Grand Canal, the Lido formed a natural barrier between the city and the Adriatic Sea. Gondolas and, later, steam or motor-boats (vaporetta) ferried visitors from the city, across the lagoon to the landing place of Santa Maria Elisabetta de Lido, near the seventeenth-century church of the same name. Venetians came for the pleasant bathing in the Adriatic, the fine sandy beaches and the fresh air. And not much else, for the desolate sands and unspoilt meadows just a few miles from the densely built oppression of the city were all part of the appeal. Lord Byron, who moved into the Palazzo Mocenigo in 1818, had four of his horses shipped over to the Lido so he could gallop along the sandy beach in the mornings. It was a chance to escape his celebrity – at least until word got out and admirers began to congregate at the Lido beach hoping to spot him.

By the 1850s, the establishment of a 'stabilimenti', with bathing facilities to cater for visitors to the island, began to slowly acknowledge the Lido's potential as a holiday destination in its own right. Travelling to the Lido on a Monday was a tradition adopted by the city's inhabitants, who enjoyed their weekly 'Luni di Lio'. It could hardly be described as rapid or conscious resort development. An article of 1888 in The Graphic still enthused about the Lido's unspoilt qualities and recommended it as a refreshing change to Venice. But it also warned, 'It does not expect to entertain visitors; and the pedestrian who astonishes its copper-coloured fisher-folk, their wives and multitudinous children, by appearing in their midst will be hard set for a meal.'

This slow encroachment had its critics, among them the novelist Henry James, who labelled the increasing numbers of restaurants and bathing huts a 'cockney village', clearly irritated that the unspoilt idyll he first visited in 1869 had changed in the intervening four decades. James was writing at the time the

LIDO

Lido's two premier hotels had been built – a move that was to transform the Lido into an upmarket destination of international renown. In 1908, the Excelsior Palace Hotel opened with a fanfare and a huge beach party of 3,000 people – an inauguration in keeping with the hotel's size and scale. It was the brainchild of Nicolò Spada, founder of the Italian hotel group CIGA. Spada, mindful no doubt of the growing popularity of the French Riviera resorts, hoped to lure those with wealth, status, taste and talent to Venice. With the support of politician and businessman Giuseppe Volpi he earmarked the Lido as the place that could offer leisure and luxury just a short boat trip away from a city crammed with art and culture. Shaped into something more tailored to the high-class tourist's tastes, the Lido could offer the best of both worlds.

Spada engaged the architect Giovanni Sardi who, given a seemingly limitless budget, created an extravaganza of a building that melded traditional Venetian neo-Gothic with a Moorish flavour. Its public spaces, from the huge ballroom encrusted with plasterwork *putti* to the Taverna restaurant with its Romanesque archways, were devoted to providing comfort alongside conviviality, and its location, right on the beach, encouraged an easy informality. By the 1920s, as the 'sunbaskers' of the beach came in for lunch, it was an unwritten rule that they would dine in bathing costumes, covered only by a *peignoir* or beach pyjamas – the uniform of the fashionable Lido set. Mabel Howard, writing about Lido fashions in *The Sketch* magazine in 1927 confirmed the trend, telling readers:

> At luncheon everyone drifts towards La Taverna, and, to protect the head from the noonday sun, many wear those fascinating rush hats with fringed edges that children rejoice in over here. Pyjamas are, of course, still de rigueur – in fact, I doubt if anyone would dare to commit the impropriety of wearing a skirt at lunch!

The Grand Hôtel des Bains, opened in 1909, was built by Francesco Masioli in a restrained, classical style, and less flamboyant than the Excelsior. Compared to the sybarites at the Excelsior Palace, the Grand Hôtel des Bains attracted a slightly older clientele. It was here that Thomas Mann stayed and was inspired to write *Death in Venice*. It was also favoured by Diaghilev who, five years after he had browsed through Cecil Beaton's sketches in St Mark's Square, breathed his last in his room at the hotel.

With two flagship luxury hotels firmly established, more building and development took place, including two more family-orientated hotels, the

Brochure cover for the Venice Lido from 1935 with a couple taking a civilised cup of tea under the striped awning of their beach capanna. (Mary Evans Picture Library)

◄ Group of bathers relaxing outside a *capanna*, 1926. The most exclusive, and therefore most expensive, *capannas* were located on the Excelsior Palace's private beach. (Süddeutsche Zeitung Photo/Mary Evans)

◄ Lazing at the Lido. Dorothy Caruso, widow of the Italian tenor Enrico Caruso, pictured on the beach at the Venice Lido with her second husband, Captain Ernest Ingram, and her children, Gloria and baby Jacqueline, who enjoys the Lido way of life from the comfort of her crib. (© Illustrated London News/ Mary Evans)

Grand Hotel Lido and the Hotel Villa Regina. The authorities were careful to ensure building was carried out sensitively, with many villas designed in the Liberty style – a Venetian riff on art nouveau. Meanwhile, an attempt by the leader of the Futurist movement, Filippo Marinetti, to promote rails and roads between the laguna's islands, including the Lido, was firmly quashed by the *antipontisti*, who were committed to preserving the unique character and history of the lagoon city and its satellite islands. This careful development paid dividends. In the years following the First World War, the Lido was to become a popular alternative for travellers seeking a change from the French Riviera. It attracted a cosmopolitan mix of aristocrats and celebrities who were labelled the 'Setiembres' due to their preference for late August and September visits. This was particularly true of the British visitors as it not only coincided with the end of the season in London, but temperatures by this time of year had bearably mellowed.

Each year, in early autumn, the society magazines were full of news from the Lido: the fun, the fashions, the faces. Of the latter, some of the familiar figures of Venetian society included Baroness d'Erlanger, giver of that 1926 costume ball, and her daughter Baba. Baba's petite frame and intense, petulant gaze could often be spotted among groups of affluent sun worshippers – and she was always, without exception, impeccably dressed. Another regular was Iya, Lady Abdy – a majestic blonde figure of over 6 feet with a regal Russian countenance, whose home, the Palazzo Pizzani on the Grand Canal, frequently provided an elegant background to the press photographs she posed for. There was the neat, spare figure of Doris Castlerosse, her chic appearance belying her appetite for taking numerous lovers, and the glamorous Countess Andrea di Robilant, the former ballet dancer Kyra Alanova. Princess Jane di San Faustino, an American who married into one of Italy's oldest aristocratic families and dressed almost exclusively in white, was behind one of the highlights of the Venetian calendar: an extravagant annual charity fête. There was Lady Mendl, formerly Elsie de Wolfe, the interior designer who, at the age of 60, had married Sir Charles Mendl and was name-checked by Cole Porter in *Anything Goes*. Princesse Edmond de Polignac, formerly Winnaretta Singer, heiress of the Singer sewing-machine empire and aunt of the terribly chic Daisy Fellowes, was a generous and involved patron of the arts. Her amicable marriage of convenience meant she engaged in a number of relationships with women including the painter Romaine Brooks and Olga de Meyer, wife of the photographer Baron Adolph de Meyer and another key member of the Venice set.

It was a heady brew of fame, talent, style and notoriety, and by the early 1930s Cecil Beaton himself, previously on the periphery of this hallowed circle, was listed in the society magazines in the same breath as the celebrities whose patronage he had once craved. One photograph shows him with Lady Abdy on the beach by one of the Lido's famous *capanna* (a sort of tented beach cabin unique to the Lido); in another shot, he sits with Elsa Maxwell, wearing a fez at a rakish angle.

The American Elsa Maxwell emerged during the 1920s as an influential figure of the Venice Lido and Monte Carlo, and could number Cole Porter, Noël Coward and the Prince of Wales among her friends and acquaintances. A composer, pianist, actress, social fixer, party-giver and publicist, she cannot be missed among the press photographs of society littering the pages of magazines at the

'The Playground of the Queen of the Adriatic": opulence taking its ease at the "Taverna" on the Lido', by Fortunino Matania, *The Graphic*, 18 June 1927. Casual dress was the order of the day at the Taverna restaurant of the Excelsior Palace: 'In the course of many seasons, the luncheon hour has become a social function at which all the latest bathing creations from Paris and Vienna are displayed before the eyes of fashionable Europe and America; for with the possible exception of Deauville, the Lido is the most cosmopolitan, as well as one of the youngest of summer resorts.' (© Illustrated London News Ltd/Mary Evans)

time. A short, dumpy figure (by her own admission, she claimed to be totally uninterested in fashion), her appearance was in refreshingly marked contrast to the groomed, sylph-like beauties she invited to her parties.

With a bulging address book, and an innate instinct for networking at the highest level, her high-spirited and irrepressible character saw her forge a career out of bringing society together and making sure the papers knew about it. She relied on a number of well-connected, wealthy friends to keep her solvent, including her long-term friend, the Scottish heiress and singer Dickie Fellowes-Gordon, and operated on a barter system with hotels and restaurants. She brought the customers and the publicity and, in return, the hotel managers took care of the bill. It was a successful business arrangement, for wherever Elsa Maxwell sprinkled her magic party dust, customers, enhanced reputations and profits inevitably followed.

The Bystander, listing some of the key personalities at resorts around Europe in 1935, wrote with a typical tongue in cheek that Maxwell was a 'resort queen in excelsis, may be met anywhere, animating anything. Expected simultaneously in New York, the Ritz Bar, the Riviera, the Sahara, the Adriatic and the Baltic. Should be offered Balkan crown at any moment.' Her reputation for throwing original parties was legendary. In 1930, *The Sketch*, reported on the forthcoming 'Bal au Contraire' in Venice organised by Maxwell and Dickie Gordon, in which guests were asked to come as their opposite. 'Miss Maxwell has such a decided *flair* for this sort of gay gathering, her parties always go with a swing!' raved the magazine.

In her memoirs, Maxwell claimed she was approached by the Mayor of Venice who asked for help in transforming the Lido's fortunes in the early 1920s. How, he wondered, could the city attract wealthy male visitors, particularly Americans? Maxwell advised that a golf course could and should be built near the coast at Alberone and recommended the British professional Phil May map out a ten-hole course. She added that motor-boat races would also lure the right sort of affluence. Added to these attractions, in 1927 Count Volpi also arranged for the Lido to become one of the venues for the prestigious Schneider Trophy air race. If this wasn't enough to attract the A-list, then the nightlife on offer was as sophisticated as any that might be found in Paris, New York or London. 'The extraordinary fascination of the Lido is largely due to its combination of simple and sophisticated delights', concluded *The Sketch* in 1928, 'while at night the chic world dons its smartest costumes to dine and dance in the smart restaurants or appears in fancy dress at the various important fêtes which take place during the season.'

◄◄ Keeping cool on the tennis court: Miss S.T. Phillips has a game in her bathing suit. Those staying at the Venice Lido regularly went from beach to tennis court in swimwear. (© Illustrated London News/Mary Evans)

◄ Royalty at the Lido, 1932. The Prince of Wales with his brother Prince George, the future Duke of Kent, at the Lido beach at Venice, where they stopped off during a Mediterranean trip. The princes' appearance caused quite a stir among the usually laconic denizens of the Lido. They are pictured here with Captain Alistair Mackintosh. (© Illustrated London News/Mary Evans)

The long tradition of Venetian carnival was appropriated by visitors to the city, who delighted in dressing up for costume balls. Baroness d'Erlanger's ball was just one of many. Later that season, a fête on the theme of 'Chinese Fantasies in Venice of the Eighteenth Century' was organised by the artist and designer Umberto Brunelleschi and held at the Excelsior Palace. Brunelleschi's illustrations graced the pages of prestigious magazines such as *Gazette du Bon Ton*, and he would later design costumes for the Casino de Paris, Folies Bergère and the celebrated Josephine Baker. His was a name to reckon with. The marketing teams behind the Venice Lido made sure to mention it when advertising the entertainment on offer. In 1933, at Princess Jane di San Faustino's annual charity gala, the ballet of choice was *L'Après-Midi d'un Faune*, renowned for its strident eroticism. Performed by Serge Lifar and Brigit Hartwig, it would have pleased the worldly and open-minded audience.

Such events were one of the highlights of a stay at the Lido. A programme to the Venetian summer of 1935 lists a mouth-watering array of delights for the culture vulture. There were several art exhibitions including a Titian blockbuster; the seventh International Motor-Boat Race; tennis tournaments at the Tennis Club on the Lido as well as a firework display over the sea; an open-air performance of *The Merchant of Venice*; and a summer feast at the Lido. There was also a 'Full Moon Festival' in St Mark's Square, 'with rhythmical dances'; a regatta for gondolas; a 'Night-Festival' on the Grand Canal where the palaces, bridges and *traghetti* were illuminated and musicians performed

▶ Linda Lee Thomas (1883–1954), American socialite and the wife of musical theatre composer Cole Porter. They are pictured at the Venice Lido in 1926, where she and Cole regularly holidayed and were centre of the social milieu, renting palaces, hosting dance parties and courting some of the period's most prominent creative figures. (© Illustrated London News/Mary Evans)

▶ ▶ Cecil Beaton pictured with renowned party-giver and publicist Elsa Maxwell at the Lido in 1933. Just seven years after he had visited Venice as an ingénue photographer hoping to break into the inner sanctum of fashionable society, Beaton had himself become as famous as many of his sitters. Maxwell, 'resort queen in excelsis', claimed to be instrumental in establishing the Venice Lido as one of the world's leading luxury destinations during the 1920s. (© Illustrated London News/Mary Evans)

upon the water; a fashion show at the Excelsior Palace; and a historical regatta on the Grand Canal. At the latter, the city's residents whose homes lined the canal festooned windows with colourful curtains and tapestries, completing the vision of renaissance glory.

Spectacle went hand in hand with culture in Venice as the city's impossibly picturesque architecture and waterways provided a readymade backdrop for performances. In 1925, Dame Nellie Melba gave an impromptu performance from a gondola in the middle of the Grand Canal. 'Things like that happen in Venice', wrote Cecil Roberts in *The Sphere*, though other reports claimed the periodic chugging of the passing *vaporetta* played havoc with the acoustics. The Venice Biennale began in 1895, when the International Exhibition of Contemporary Art held an exhibition in the sumptuous rooms at the Café Florian, and continues to this day. In 1938, among the pieces of work on display was a statue of Countess Barbara Hutton by Antonio Berti, owned by Count Volpi – an appropriate subject as Hutton was a frequent visitor to Venice and the Lido.

By the early 1930s, the new phenomenon of 'talkies' prompted Volpi to extend the city's cultural agency with a film festival on the Lido. At the very first Venice Film Festival in 1932, a screening of *Grand Hotel*, based on the novel by Vicki

◄ Society at play. Theatre designer and interior decorator Oliver Messel, Mme Lucien Lelong (Princess Natalie Paley) and the Ballets Russes star Serge Lifar pose for a photograph against a stage set constructed of sand at the Venice Lido. (© Illustrated London News/Mary Evans)

◄ Couples dancing at sea on a *gallegiante* in 1925. Behind them, the imposing Moorish façade of the Excelsior Palace looks over the Adriatic Sea. (Süddeutsche Zeitung Photo/ Mary Evans)

Baum and starring Greta Garbo, took place on the terrace of the Excelsior with an A-list audience that 'might have been taken from a Cochran first-nighter', according to *The Tatler*. Among those present were Lady Cunard, Lady Mendl, Lady Castlerosse, Oliver Messel, Cecil Beaton, Tilly Losch, the Mosleys, the Duff Coopers, Bob Boothby and Brendon Bracken.

The striving for artistic spectacle extended to the Lido's nightspots. At the Excelsior Palace's Chez Vous nightclub guests could dine under the stars against a backdrop of luminous, rainbow-hued fountains, while enjoying some of the period's best cabaret turns. These ranged from Leslie Hutchinson's jazz band to a 19-year-old dancer called Mary Corday, who, during the 1926 season, demonstrated the Charleston, pulling diners from their chairs to attempt the steps. Included among her 'volunteers' was the Prince of Kapurthala, much to the delight and rapturous applause of the audience.

When available, adventurous dancing couples could venture out on to the *gallegiante* – a kind of floating raft with a dance floor, the corners of which were finished to look like the prow or stern of a gondola. Lit up by Venetian lamps that cast a glow over the dancers and the sea beyond, it must have been a magical experience to dance the foxtrot upon the gentle waves. The *gallegiante* was the idea of Cole Porter and his wife Linda. The couple, both independently wealthy, travelled annually to the Lido and were among Venice's most original and popular party-givers, Cole Porter being recognisable by the Stetson he frequently wore.

Elsewhere, specially constructed supper pavilions studded with 'fairy lanterns' elevated the experience of al fresco dining to a new level and, in the Turkish Bar, patrons could enjoy a post-dip refreshment while lazing on a chaise lounge, strewn with silk cushions, exotic rugs and throws. Many evenings were spent hopping between Venice and the Lido, such was the convenience and frequency of the *vaporetta*, which could ferry people back and forth between the two in just ten minutes. A pre-prandial cocktail might first be in order at Florian's, the famous 300-year-old bar in St Mark's Square, after which dinner at Danieli's or the Luna. The Luna Restaurant was an outpost of London's fashionable Embassy nightclub run by Luigi Naintre, whose brother-in-law Bresciano was in charge in Venice. The fact that members of the Embassy in London were extra welcome made the Luna popular with British visitors, the most distinguished of whom were asked to sign the restaurant's Golden Book. Afterwards, a leisurely gondola ride along the Grand Canal might be the choice for romantics, but for those with stamina, there was still plenty of time to catch a

◄ Oswald Mosley and his wife Cynthia on holiday in Venice in happier times in 1925, in the company of Mr E.V. Strachey. On a subsequent trip in 1932, Oswald's affair with Diana Guinness (née Mitford) had become painfully obvious to everyone, including their respective spouses. (© Illustrated London News/Mary Evans)

◄ 'The Gaiety of the Lido on the Adriatic Shore. An Impression of Chez Vouz', by Fortunino Matania, *The Sphere*, 25 June 1927. Matania's view of Chez Vous gives prominence to the multi-coloured fountains forming a magical backdrop to the dance floor. He also included a few famous faces, including the painter Philip de László and Lady Diana Duff-Cooper, seated at the table in the foreground wearing a pink dress. (© Illustrated London News/ Mary Evans)

motor launch outside Danieli's and hop over to the Lido for more cocktails, cabaret and dancing into the early hours. There was always tomorrow to sleep off a hangover at the beach.

And the beach was an art in itself for seasoned Lido-ites. The 1920s ushered in the era of suntanning for holidaymakers. For centuries, pale skin had been, for Europeans, a sign of good breeding while tanned skin was the mark of the working man. Now, fashion suddenly dictated that 'sunburn' was a sign of style, status, good health and leisure. In 1932, when Sir Oswald Mosley and his wife Cynthia ('Cimmie') visited the Lido (the same year they were spotted at the first film festival), *The Tatler* reported on how they '… like nearly all the rest of the Lido population, devote hours of homage to the great god tan'.

As well as topping up his tan that year, Mosley was also devoting time to seducing Diana Guinness, formerly Mitford, who would eventually become his second wife. Their affair had become quite clear to everyone else at the Lido, including their respective spouses. One evening, Mosley asked Bob Boothby, a friend and fellow politician, to vacate his hotel room so he could use it. Boothby acquiesced and ended up sleeping in the Mosleys' *capanna* on the beach.

Capanna, or cabanas – the equivalent of a British beach hut, though more tent-like – could be hired for a week or a whole season. Those on the front row of the private beach at the Excelsior were the most desirable, and friends frequently shared a pitch. Here, a day could be spent dipping in and out of the warm waters, lying in the sun or shade as desired, on loungers or mattresses draped with an arrangement of exotic rugs and throws. If the short walk to the Taverna for lunch was too much effort, then local costers patrolled the beach selling fresh figs and peaches on trays. For those with the energy to do so, the Excelsior's geranium-coloured tennis courts offered the chance to work off a spaghetti luncheon. Nobody was expected to change into tennis clothes; most served and volleyed in their bathing costumes.

In August 1932, there was a flurry of excitement when the Prince of Wales and his brother, Prince George, appeared at the Lido en route to Corfu. Arriving by the Orient Express, they checked into the Excelsior, appearing on the beach fifteen minutes later. *The Sketch* described the reactions of the usually unflappable colony of Lido habitués:

it was more than human nature could stand not to try and catch a glimpse of him. So, to be honest, the occupants of nearly every capanna wandered down in the direction of the capanna set aside for the Prince. It was

The Lure of the Lido

After the dip the sip: smart
Society in becoming undress
forgathers at the Turkish Bar

*Sunshine and laughter, care-free days and soft Italian
nights, the sparkling Adriatic, gay pyjamas and a
general spirit of joyous goodwill—these are but a few
of the impressions which the Lido leaves on those
that have experienced its delights. The playground
of the western world lays its lovely shore at the feet
of Society, and Society asks for nothing better than to
bathe, laze, and dance the hours away. Bathing and
dancing are the main activities, the latter taking place
on the terrace of the Hotel Excelsior, or, after dark,
at "Chez Vous," its entrancing open-air ballroom*

amusing also, to see the life-guards firmly standing by in their boat, for if there's a safe beach in the world, it is that of the Lido; but, after all, the safety of so popular a Prince has to be safeguarded in every way.

Despite the sophistication of the Lido's visitors, there was an almost regressive, child-like quality to life on the beach. In advertisements and magazine columns the Lido was constantly referred to as 'society's playground' and the relaxed dress code of pyjamas and swimwear only added to the resort's cosseted, hedonistic character. In 1931, the designer Oliver Messel held a competition to build sandcastles, though their scale and standard were rather superior to any usually achieved with a humble bucket and spade. Messel struck an artistic pose, along with Madame Lucien Lelong, the former Natalie Paley, wife of the French couturier and the Ballets Russes star Serge Lifar, the trio theatrically presenting his sandy creation complete with baroque swag reliefs worthy of any stage. If there is a metaphor for the Lido's easy synthesis of fun, hedonism and culture, perhaps Messel's sandy stage set is it.

Writing about the Lido in its travel pages in 1926, *The Sphere* magazine summed up the care-free existence that made it such a unique experience for those lucky enough to enjoy it:

You may roll about in these waters the whole day long, varying the programme with visits to the café-terraces that overlook the sands. You may frolic as you like, and live as you like. And if your frolics, your dress, and your mode of living has something bizarre about it, so much the better. The Lido will like you then. After all, why not be a little different, a little barbaric, for a few weeks in the year?

Why not indeed?

THE PRINCE OF WALES AT HOMBURG: TAKING THE WATERS
A SKETCH AT THE ELISABETH-BRUNNEN

◄ King Edward VII, while still Prince of Wales, taking the waters of the Elisabeth-Brunnan spring at Bad Homburg in an illustration from *The Graphic*, 1 September 1894. Bertie, who had visited Homburg since 1882, took the waters at the spring named after his great-aunt at seven o'clock each morning, played tennis as part of his slimming regime and dined at the town's smart Kursaal in the evening. His patronage gave the quiet spa town fashionable status. (Mary Evans Picture Library)

Karlsbad.
Der Sprudel.

5

BADEN-BADEN

CURE WHILE YOU PLAY

'THE CURE' – WHETHER SEEKING IT, or administering it – was a serious business in the spa towns (or *Kurort*) of Germany. At Homburg, the Kaiser Wilhelm Bad, which opened in 1890, boasted fifty-two separate bathrooms in which visitors could soak away their ailments in the warm, mineral-rich water brought directly from the wells via a network of steam pipes laid underneath the rooms. In addition to this, patients could select from myriad other treatments: an inhalation room, mud baths, rooms for massage and 'douches of every description'. At Marienbad, *The Bystander* magazine of August 1913 reported that every shop and public place came equipped with a weighing chair to motivate visitors to keep walking everywhere, as ordered by doctors. 'To thin or not to thin is the [Marienbad] question,' it warned, 'and comparisons of weights and what one may and may not eat is the prevalent shop as much as the roulette and its numbers at Monte Carlo.' Frequented by King Edward VII in his later years, the rotund Bertie tried unsuccessfully to taper the waist that had earned him the nickname 'Tum-Tum' by partaking of Marienbad's gaseous water, thought to be efficacious for slimming.

In Carlsbad in West Bohemia (now Karlovy in the Czech Republic), queues for taking the spring waters began to form as early as 4 a.m. daily, and by 6 a.m. some 10,000 people would have assembled to fill their glasses, attached via a strap to their person. Sometimes, the lines leading up to each of the eighteen springs could be up to 1 mile long. In March 1901, the discovery of a second spring, or 'Sprudel',

'Der Sprudel' in Carlsbad. The discovery of the spa town's second spring in 1901, ten times larger than the original, drew even more visitors seeking the cure. The spring threw an estimated 8,000 litres of health-giving water into the air every minute. (Mary Evans Picture Library)

THE GRAND CLUB-HOUSE (KURHAUS) AT BADEN.

◄ The *Kurhaus* or 'Conversation House' in Baden-Baden, from *The Illustrated News of the World*, 1858. The Conversation House was the nineteenth-century equivalent of a combined arts centre and entertainment complex, offering spaces for reading, dancing, cards, refreshments, concerts and gambling. (Mary Evans Picture Library)

was the cause of much celebration among Carlsbaders. Ten times larger than the original, it hurled 8,000 litres of water per minute into the air with an impressive forcefulness that was bound to draw more visitors to the town.

And come they did. In 1900, Carlsbad welcomed 50,000 invalids, hoping to ease a variety of ailments, whether aching joints or hacking coughs, as well as 108,000 comparatively healthy tourists and travellers. The beautiful Black Forest town of Baden-Baden boasted annual visitors exceeding 70,000, who came to sit in steaming sulphur baths, swallow the hot waters in the specially constructed Trinkhalle or sweat it out in Turkish baths. Such penitent activity was balanced by myriad amusements to rival any other resort. With one marketing slogan commanding visitors to 'Cure While You Play', Baden-Baden aimed to lift the spirits as well as heal the body.

The writer Eugene Guilt, who wrote *A Summer in Baden-Baden* in 1853, declared, 'Europe has only two capitals: in the winter, Paris; in the summer,

Baden-Baden.' Situated in the south-west German duchy of Baden- Württemberg, Baden-Baden nestles in a typically German landscape of dark, pine-covered hills, sparkling rivers, waterfalls and mysterious rocky outcrops and grottoes. Yet it owed its success as a fashionable resort to the French.

A short distance from the French border, Baden (as it was then known) became a place of refuge for French aristocrats fleeing the revolution at the end of the eighteenth century. When the political upheaval turned out to be more than temporary, many French émigrés settled there. Some established shops selling luxury items such as fragrance and silks, catering to the yearly increase in wealthy visitors who came for the cure. The marriage of Stéphanie de Beauharnais, the adopted daughter of Napoleon Bonaparte, to Grand Duke Karl of Baden, was not particularly successful, but further infused Baden-Baden with a French aura as the Grand Duchess was a regular visitor.

It was the French too who developed Baden-Baden's reputation as a centre for gambling. Antoine Chabert, from nearby Strasbourg, opened a casino in 1824 in the town's *Kurhaus*, or Conversation House. The Conversation House catered to all tastes, offering spaces for reading, dancing, cards, refreshments, concerts and gambling. The gaming saloon, with its red, coffered ceiling hung with glittering chandeliers, was particularly seductive. Chabert established a habit among visitors for taking coffee in the late afternoon, no doubt aware that providing them with a caffeine boost would extend their stamina for remaining at the gaming tables each evening. He also invited the virtuoso violinist Niccolò Paganini to play at the casino – a formula of marrying musical excellence with commercial venture that still exists in similar form at Las Vegas today.

Antoine Chabert's reign at Baden-Baden ended when another Frenchman, Jacques Bénazet, arrived at a time when gambling was banned in France. Seeing an opportunity in Baden-Baden, he outbid Chabert for the franchise and set about investing heavily in Baden-Baden's infrastructure while finding enterprising ways to publicise the resort. A railway branch line from Oos delivered guests straight into the town centre, whereas previously they had travelled the final few miles of the journey by carriage. A racecourse just outside the town at Iffezheim was founded by Jacques' son, Édouard, in 1858, whose starry membership, including Edward VII when Prince of Wales, soon established the course as one of the most fashionable on the international racing circuit. During the Bénazet years, distinguished visitors were encouraged to pay a visit to the photographer Jean-François Utz's studio to officially document their patronage of the spa. And, as music was such a fundamental ingredient in a spa resort's appeal, Bénazet

◄ Taking the waters was a serious business in central Europe. Spa guests at Carlsbad pictured by photographer Alois Beer in 1895, with their traditional drinking cup (Imagno/Mary Evans)

ensured the town's band increased in size to become a world-class orchestra, therefore enticing musical titans such as Berlioz and Liszt to play there. Several magnificent baths were built, including the majestic Friedrichsbad, opened in 1877, aiming to emulate the great baths of Caracalla or Diocletian. The Landesbad followed in 1888 and the Augustabad in 1890. Visitors suffering from respiratory diseases could receive specialist treatment at the Inhalatorium, in which a pervading scent of pine needles gave clogged-up airways a good spring clean.

Journalists were invited on all-expenses-paid trips to the spa town and, in return, they unwaveringly waxed lyrical in their reviews. This publicity drive, together with a consistent programme of improvements, saw Baden-Baden's popularity grow steadily throughout the nineteenth century. 'The whole area abounds in the most exquisite rides, drives and walks through the pine woods,' enthused *The Traveller* magazine in 1900. A few months later, it published a photograph of the town's English chaplain, Rev. J. Archibald S. White, with his two daughters gliding around Baden-Baden's skating meadow. Rev. White was 'a most enthusiastic artistic skater', it reported, being quick to reassure readers concerned they may end up mixing with undesirables: 'There is not the slightest fear of the visitors to the rink being other than select, as the admission is by ticket only.'

No 'summer capital' was complete without an avenue or promenade in which to idly saunter in one's finery, and Baden-Baden's Lichtentaler Allee, lined with oaks and chestnut trees, provided a perfect and very picturesque opportunity. Many of Baden-Baden's most sociable buildings lined this route: the Conversation House, the Trinkhalle with its impressive colonnaded walkway, theatres, private villas and hotels, including the Hotel Stephanie, named after the town's first French Grand Duchess and styling itself as the 'hotel of the English aristocracy'. The nearby Badischer Hof Hotel – the first grand hotel to have been built in Baden-Baden in 1809 – had its own *badehaus* with thirty polished stone tubs and even a thermal bath for horses. Up in the hills above the town, Dr Dengler's Sanatorium offered a more strictly regimented cure away from the temptations of rich restaurant menus and late-night gambling. The Dengler regime was effective. *The Bystander* noted the immense frame of the aristocratic journalist Lord Castlerose had noticeably diminished by four or five stone after a visit to this 'most severe disciplinarian' in 1932. Guests were allowed to come into town once a week to let their hair down, doubtless undoing all of the previous week's good work.

Refined, aristocratic and seamlessly well-run, Baden-Baden's fortunes were to waver in the aftermath of the First World War as hyperinflation and economic

◀ Tea on the lawns outside Baden-Baden's golf club. In 1911, Baden-Baden's authorities, aware of the lucrative opportunities associated with golf, were determined to put the town on the map as a destination for the sport. An open championship was launched, with accommodation and food available free to competitors, and impressive cash prizes. (Pharcide/Mary Evans)

▶ Smart racegoers in their finery at Baden-Baden. The racecourse was founded by Edouard Bénazet in 1858 at Iffezheim, just a few miles from the spa town. Among its members was the Prince of Wales, the future King Edward VII. Illustration by Horvatij, *Meggendorfer Blatter*, 1912. (Mary Evans Picture Library)

◀ One of the charms of Baden-Baden was the outdoor shopping experience in the Kurgarten – the park in front of the *Kurhaus*. Vendors laid out their wares on tables or opened up their shop fronts, enabling visitors to peruse in pleasant conditions. Illustration by Reginald Cleaver, *The Graphic*, 31 July 1909. (© Illustrated London News/Mary Evans)

◀ A crowd greets the Führer in front of von Brenner's Stephanie Hotel, Baden-Baden, on 25 September 1935. The town enjoyed privileged status for a brief period during the 1930s, when a casino was allowed to operate and the town centre was declared *Baumeile* (a neutral zone). For Jews, it offered a comparatively safe haven, but all that was to change from 1936 onwards. (Mary Evans Picture Library)

depression produced an increasingly unsettled political climate in Germany. By the mid 1920s, as the country's economy began to settle, Germany started to welcome tourists once more, in particular the Americans who were descending on Europe 'in crazy boatloads', according to F. Scott Fitzgerald. Although the fashionable elite began to turn its gaze away from the *Kurort* and focus instead on Berlin, Baden-Baden benefited from the capital's cultural overspill. The Kurshaustheater hosted avant-garde performers from Berlin such as Hin und Zurück, which included Mahagonny-Songspiel, the first collaboration between Bertolt Brecht and Kurt Weill; the initial proposal to have two female performers in the nude was thought too risqué for Baden-Baden and promptly vetoed!

This vibrant period for art and culture was to be overshadowed by the ominous rise of the Nazi Party and Adolf Hitler. In August 1929, Foreign Minister and former Chancellor of the Weimar Republic Gustav Stresemann visited Baden-Baden to take the cure. Sadly, its curative waters could not help him and he died of a stroke in October that year, at the age of just 51. The pragmatic Stresemann was regarded as one of the last remaining politicians who might lead Germany back from the brink of extremist politics, but his death opened the gates for the dictatorship and totalitarian regime that followed. The Wall Street Crash of 1929 was also to have repercussions throughout the world, and, significantly for Baden-Baden, it meant the dwindling of a valuable source of overseas wealth.

Jewish visitors had always formed a large proportion of Baden-Baden's annual intake and were greatly valued by the business owners of the town. When the Nazis came to power in the 1930s, growing anti-Semitism in many spa resorts, especially those in the more right-wing southern areas of Germany, made it clear that Jewish custom was no longer welcome.

Both Hermann Göring and Joseph Goebbels were fond of Baden-Baden – Göring, who liked the high life, especially so. But spas, with their cosmopolitan mix of visitors and connotations of louche, immoral lifestyles, were diametrically at odds with Nazi principles. For a time, Baden-Baden was the exception. It remained immune to the rampant Nazification spreading through the rest of the country and, under its appointed *Kreisleiter* (County Leader), Kurt Bürkle, was granted permission to re-open its casino. It was an unprecedented decision under the Nazi regime and one founded on the argument that Baden-Baden's economic future depended on it. Thus economics were allowed to override Nazi ideology and make Baden-Baden one of the few places in 1930s Germany where, temporarily at least, Jews were able to live or to visit in peace. The town centre was declared *Baumeile* – a neutral zone – meaning it was safe and no political displays or demonstrations could take place there. Baden-Baden's special privileges were to make it a showcase for apparent German tolerance and hospitality. It is notable that quality British magazines like *The Bystander* frequently carried advertisements for the town during this time – a signifier of the heavy investment Germany was making to attract tourists to its 'calling card' spa town.

The upper-class British tourists returned. In 1934, *The Bystander* reported that the novelist Barbara Cartland was finishing off her latest novel, *A Beggar Wished*, at Dr Dengler's Home in Baden-Baden. Four years earlier, during the season of 1930, among the British celebrities enjoying Baden-Baden's charms were the actress Faith Celli and band leader Roy Fox. In 1936, as an adjunct to the Berlin Olympics, and with Hitler's blessing, the town played host to an international golf tournament. It was designed, like the Games, to show Germany's sporting prowess, but was inadvertently won by a British pair, T.J. Thirsk and A.L. Bentley. Joachim von Ribbentrop was forced to make a panicked journey to meet Hitler who was en route to present the prize to the assumed Aryan victors. When the Führer heard who had actually won, he turned round and headed back to Berlin.

That same year, Pamela Murray was reporting in *The Bystander* on 'Social and Sunny' Baden-Baden, and listed a number of high-profile British visitors. Lord Carnarvon was taking the cure at Dengler's, while other Brits included

RINNE
Spiel
in
BADEN
BADEN
Kunstdruckerei Künstlerbund Karlsruhe A G., Karlsruhe

Lord Eustace Percy, the son of the Duke of Northumberland, with his wife, and Mrs Ronnie Greville, the socialite, philanthropist and close confidante of the British royal family. She also noted that the leader of society, or 'Queen of Baden', Frau Richard Haniel, wife of the racehorse owner was 'a great friend of the Führer'.

'This is a darling little place, clean with a sunny spotlessness peculiar to Germany, peaceful as a health resort should be and bubbling with quiet merriment, also warm, curative waters.' With the benefit of hindsight, Murray's words appear incredibly naïve. As it was, 1936 marked the end for Baden-Baden's immunity, after which its Jewish community was given the choice of leaving or, if they stayed, handing over their businesses to Aryans. Soon, Jews were banned from the baths and were prevented from walking in the park – hard-line discrimination that was to prompt letters of complaint from Baden-Baden businessmen.

When Jewish people and their property were the subject of widespread violence on the night of 9–10 November, in what would be known as Kristallnacht, Baden-Baden did not escape. The synagogue was burned and local Jewish men rounded up and marched to Oos railway station, where they were deported to Dachau. They returned some weeks later, but to a much-changed town. Visitor numbers to the resort began to decline. One report on Baden-Baden for 1938 claimed visitors to the spa 'have greatly depleted'. Baden-Baden's Hotel Frankfurter continued to doggedly advertise in British magazines as late as 16 September 1939, its description careful to mention that the owner's wife was English.

A site of hydrotherapy since Roman times, and a fashionable resort since the nineteenth century, Baden-Baden's architecture survived the war intact and it soon began to rebuild its tourist industry. It continues to operate as a spa town today. Many of its buildings, such as the Friedrichsbad, remain in use and the pretty buildings, together with the imposing scenery, bring to mind William Makepeace Thackeray's description of Baden-Baden in his 1855 novel *The Newcomes*:

So they travelled by the accustomed route to the prettiest town of all places, where pleasure has set up her tents: Baden-Baden, and where the gay, the melancholy, the idle or occupied, grave or naughty, come for amusement, or business, or relaxation; where London beauties, having danced and flirted all the season, may dance and flirt a little more.

◄ Stylish poster advertising Baden-Baden's casino during the 1930s. The town's energetic marketing campaign during the decade sought to draw visitors from the rest of Europe and America. (Spiel in Baden-Baden (Gamble in Baden-Baden), 1938, Felix Rinne, Kunstlerdruckerei Künstlerbund Karlsruhe AG, Karlsruhe, 84 x 120cm, Galleria L'IMAGE, Alassio)

6

EGYPT

LAND OF SUNLIT GRANDEUR

IN 2018, IT TAKES UNDER FIVE HOURS to fly from London to Cairo. At the beginning of the twentieth century it could take travellers anything up to sixteen days, depending on the route. The North German Lloyd Line took five days from Marseilles, or a shorter voyage could be achieved by picking up the same boat at Naples, though it would take several days to reach either of those cities for travellers from England. An alternative could be the Orient Express from Paris to Venice, after which it was four days by sea to Alexandria. In 1924, the P&O Line sailed directly from Tilbury to Port Said taking twelve days. Compared to Biarritz or the French Riviera, getting to Egypt was certainly a more ambitious undertaking, but it was hardly a journey exclusive to hard-bitten, intrepid explorers. Ships were well equipped, provided excellent food and entertainment, and the length of the journey only required passengers to have time and money, both of which they had in abundance. Egypt may have been a different continent and a different culture, but for the tourist, it offered all the comforts of home.

In terms of climate – a national obsession for the British, then as now – Egypt was without rival, at least for the months from October to April which marked the Cairo social season. 'What is wanting in scenery is more than made up for by the air,' enthused *The Traveller* magazine in January 1901, 'I have travelled four continents without meeting such air as is breathed on the Nile.' In December 1903, *The Bystander* reported that Princess Henry of Battenberg,

◄ Poster extolling Egypt's 'perfect climate' – also the perfect way to lure holidaymakers from northern Europe. (Egypt, 1909, Augustus Osborne Lamplough, Causton, London, 100 x 73.8cm, Galleria L'IMAGE, Alassio)

◄ A photograph in front of Egypt's famous monuments was an essential part of the Egyptian experience, whether royalty or a Thomas Cook tourist. Here, Crown Prince Wilhelm of Prussia, eldest son of the Kaiser, is pictured with his wife Cecilie during a trip to Giza in the 1900s. Riding on mules, led by young Bedouins, behind them is the Sphinx and, in the background, the Menkaure pyramid (left) and the Khafre pyramid (right). (Süddeutsche Zeitung Photo/ Mary Evans)

◄ A female tourist is helped on her way up the steps of a pyramid. Illustration by Charles Wilda in *Moderne Kunst*, 1890s. (Mary Evans Picture Library)

Aufstieg auf die Pyramide.
Original-Aquarell von Charles Wilda.

Queen Victoria's youngest daughter, had arrived at the Gezirah Hotel in Cairo with her daughter Ena, the future Queen of Spain, and her youngest son Leopold. Leopold was haemophiliac and known to be a delicate child so a spell inhaling the 'clear, sparkling air' of Cairo was hoped to benefit the young Prince.

Egypt's rich heritage of ancient monuments and antiquities was another draw, turning some areas into early tourist traps. In 1869, travel pioneer Thomas Cook conducted his first customers up the Nile in one of two steamers hired by the company, the same year in which Empress Eugénie of France had attended the opening of the Suez Canal. Climbing the pyramids, particularly the Great Pyramid of Cheops, was an obligatory rite of passage for any European visitor, who would be coaxed and hoisted over the Brobdingnagian stones with the help of local guides. At the height of the season, the road from Cairo to Giza was close to gridlock as a melee of carriages, carts, donkeys and camels made their way back and forth along it. The Museum of Egyptian Antiquities in Cairo provided interest for the minority of tourists with seriously curious cultural proclivities. Subsequently, the discovery of Tutankhamen's tomb by Howard Carter in 1922 triggered a worldwide Egyptomania craze and sent another wave of visitors to Egypt, keen to immerse themselves in the excitement of one of archaeology's most important discoveries. *The Bystander* wrote in February 1923:

> The heart's desire of every visitor is to obtain permission, by fair means or foul, to enter the tomb (it is referred to now as 'THE Tomb' (tout court)); or, since that is forbidden, to peer wistfully down the entrance thereof, and perhaps, on a lucky day, to see some of the treasures carried out.

The North African sun and the romantic proximity of ancient civilisations gave Cairo a unique 'Oriental' mystique missing from European resorts. Yet in many ways, the city's social scene was as sophisticated as any in Europe, particularly during the Edwardian era. Rudyard Kipling travelled there with his wife in 1913 and described the city in a letter to his two children as 'a cross between Rome and Florence with touches of Cape Town thrown in'. R. Talbot Kelly, describing Cairo in his 1904 book on Egypt published by A. & C. Black, rather mourned the westernisation of certain areas of Cairo:

> The European quarters, though in many ways handsome, are too much like some fashionable Continental town to be altogether picturesque, though some of the older Italian streets are not without interest. All are beautified

by avenues of 'lebbek' trees (Nile acacia), and an occasional rond point, with its small ornamental garden and plashing fountain.

For anyone wanting to see the real 'Orientalism' of Cairo, he recommended hiring a donkey with a boy and exploring alone, 'without your Baedeker [guide book]'.

Cairo's multinational population included a dominant British presence from the time of the Anglo-Egyptian war in 1882 until 1936, when a treaty was finally to end the British protectorate in Egypt and, with it, decades of British influence. British troops remained until they finally withdrew in 1956, two years after the Suez Crisis. But for half a century, British civil servants, diplomats and several regiments of the British Army populated Cairo, leading society to follow and set up an Anglocentric community where things were done just the way they liked it: hotels were palatial, but also comparatively cheap; shops selling British goods catered to this colony; their spiritual welfare was attended to by the rector of

All Saints Church in Cairo. A newspaper, *The Sphinx*, was produced as reading
matter for British and Americans in the city.

Impoverished families of good standing might also choose to launch their
daughters on their first season in Cairo rather than London; Cairo, after all, had
dashing men in bountiful supply, and one could live in some style on a fraction
of what the season might cost in London. Agatha Christie spent three months
in Cairo in 1910, when she stayed at the Gezirah Palace with her mother and
attended five dances a week. Balls, dances and receptions filled each evening,
some lavish enough to warrant special mention in the press. When the Heliopolis
Palace opened in 1911, it celebrated with a magnificent inaugural ball attended
by all of Cairo society.

In the years leading up to the First World War, Lord Kitchener presided
over Egypt as British Agent and Consul-General, with some success. Then, as
now, most British visitors were poor linguists but Kitchener was notable for
being fluent in Arabic – a skill that no doubt ameliorated diplomatic relations.
A gruff misanthrope and rumoured homosexual, Lord Kitchener – he of the
glowering, accusatory Great War recruitment campaign – hardly presented
as a social butterfly and seasoned party-giver. Nevertheless, under his watch,
he held a number of elegant and well-attended garden parties, an invite to
which was considered a rubber-stamping of one's arrival into Cairo society's
inner sanctum.

In the post-war years, with the popularity of nightclubs increasing in London,
Paris and continental resorts, one of London's most exclusive nightspots, The
Embassy Club – a favourite of the Prince of Wales – opened a Cairene outpost.
Lou Preagar, the famous band leader from Ciro's and Romano's in London, spent
three winter seasons at Shepheard's Hotel during the 1920s, bringing the latest
dance tunes to the Egyptian capital. Such a social whirl required an appropriate
wardrobe, which was a subject that preoccupied the ladies' fashion column in
The Traveller magazine. It advised lady readers to remember their riding habits
when travelling to Egypt, adding, 'For the rest, the details of dress may be the
smartest of those fit for the London Season.' *The Bystander* in 1913 told readers,
'As to evening dresses, you can't have too many … remember that people are
very smart in Cairo and appear in full dress every night for dinner in the hotels.'
The magazine also recommended bringing at least one fancy-dress costume
– a regular fixture in Cairo's social calendar. 'Just now there is an epidemic of
fancy-dress dances', reported *The Sketch* a decade later, 'and this will conclude
with the big one of the season at Mena, just when the moon is full.' The amount of

luggage for a season in Cairo must have required several large trunks, followed by several large tips to Egyptian porters.

A typical day for the holidaymaker in Cairo was outlined by *The Sphere* magazine in 1911. It suggested that after dancing until 1 a.m. and then a champagne supper, visitors with enough energy to rise from their beds the next morning might walk to Thomas Cook's to draw money, and go to the photographers to see if their films were developed. After that, they could either go for a ride in the desert or else do a little bargain-hunting at the bazaar. In the latter, the British ingrained prejudice of Cairo's native residents, referred to broadly, and incorrectly, as 'Arabs', came to the fore. 'In such shops, from 20% to 50% is usually asked above the prices which will be accepted if the purchaser condescends to haggle', warned *The Traveller* magazine in 1900. 'Most English tourists being above this practice pay from 50 to 150% more than their purchase is worth.' Elsewhere there were similar grumbles about street sellers and tour guides not vetted by a hotel or travel company.

Carrying on one's day, smart society congregated for tea at the Khedivial Sports Club, where a menu of sporting facilities was on offer – lawn tennis, croquet, squash, golf and polo – catering to British tastes. At the Agency, the centre for British civil servants and diplomats in Egypt, there were concerts and bridge parties. Even a night at the opera was possible in Cairo, which had its own Khedivial Opera House, built in 1869 to celebrate the opening of the Suez Canal. Opera and perhaps dinner, dancing and champagne occupied the small hours until a new day dawned and a similar routine followed.

Much social life revolved around Cairo's grand hotels, proclaimed as 'The last word in splendour and service' by *The Graphic* in 1930. Cairo itself boasted the Semiramis Hotel, run by Mr Hein in the years leading up to the First World War. He came highly recommended by *The Bystander*'s travel correspondent, who was impressed by his efforts in arranging luncheons for guests, finding a reliable *dragoman* (guide), as well as donkeys or camels to ride. He would even engage the hotel's motorbus to ferry guests to view the pyramids bathed in moonlight.

At the Heliopolis Palace Hotel, built in 1911 in an opulent Oriental style, in addition to its 400 bedrooms, there were two restaurants on different floors, both with views across the desert. The delightful Mena House at Giza, with its raised terrace and sheltered verandah, had the rambling appearance and atmosphere of a well-run English country house, except for one thing: 'The Pyramids rise behind and above it; they actually seem in the background of the hotel', wrote *The Bystander*. For those who were not resident at Mena House, it still provided an elegant stop-off for tea with visitors to the pyramids.

Sixteen miles out of Cairo, Helouan (Helwan) could lay claim to be the oldest health resort in the world, mentioned by Arab writers as flourishing in the seventh century due to its wonder-working springs. As well as two hotels, the Grand Hôtel des Bains and the Tewfik Palace Hotel (formerly a royal palace), there were a casino and an eighteen-hole golf course. Also, it was perfectly possible to stay there but enjoy the amusements of Cairo due to the theatre train, which left the city at 12.30 a.m. in time to deposit Helouan tourists back at their hotels.

In the centre of Cairo, Shepheard's was an institution, founded in 1841 by Samuel Shepheard and originally named L'Hôtel des Anglais, though in later years it was said to be favoured by Americans (the British preferred the Savoy-Continental according to one report). Film stars, royalty and politicians all at some point had sat on the hotel's famous verandah overlooking the

street, and to sit there on its famous wicker chairs was as essential to the Cairo experience as a visit to the pyramids. A correspondent for *The Sphere* magazine admitted that on arrival in Cairo, 'we made tracks at once for Shepheard's. There were many things we wanted to do in this city of cities, and the first was to sit awhile on the famous terrace – the scene of a thousand dramas in film, fiction and reality.'

Despite the scale of these hotels, sometimes Cairo could not accommodate all its visitors and rooms ran out. In April 1901, there were reports that hotels were overflowing and were resorting to all kinds of expedient measures such as putting up guests in bathrooms or on verandahs.

◄ Tourists on a Thomas Cook tour, milling around on the famous verandah and outside the luxurious Shepheard's Hotel in Cairo. Once one of the great hotels of the world, Shepheard's was burnt to the ground during anti-British riots in 1952. (© Thomas Cook Archive/Mary Evans)

Most visitors to Egypt did not limit their stay to Cairo alone. *The Traveller*, writing at the beginning of the twentieth century, recommended, 'Perhaps the most popular plan … is to spend two or three weeks in Cairo itself, then go up the river for a month or six weeks, returning again to the city for March gaieties and to avoid the growing heat further south.' Transport further south was usually by a boat that would take passengers the 580 miles from Cairo to Assouan (Aswan), stopping at various points along the way to see Egypt's archaeological wonders. At Karnak, Luxor and other stop-off points they would be met by skilled *dragoman* guides with donkeys provided by locals and hired by Thomas Cook, whose steamers were the most popular form of transport down the Nile. After disembarking, guides would take parties to view temples, pyramids and ancient city sites, and escort them to appropriate places for lunch (Pagnon's Hotel was a popular pit stop for lunch near Luxor). For the wealthiest travellers, rather than taking a Thomas Cook steam boat, a 'few hundred pounds' would buy a *dahabeah* – a personal boat with full crew – allowing one to sail downriver at a leisurely pace, stopping whenever and wherever one fancied. This migratory pattern, whether by steamer or the more luxurious *dahabeah*, meant that many of Egypt's more southerly attractions were just as busy as Cairo and experienced the same problems. When visitor numbers exceeded capacity, desert hotels such as Mena House erected tents for guests, much to the horror of some Edwardian ladies who were no doubt cursing *The Traveller*'s suggestions about what clothing to pack. Evening dresses and fancy-dress costumes were of little use when camping in the desert.

In December 1931, Margaret Whigham, travelled to Egypt for the winter season with her parents; it was hoped the warm climate would ease Mrs Whigham's arthritis. A celebrated debutante, Margaret thoroughly enjoyed the social scene in Cairo, in particular the young officers who made willing dance partners at the endless round of dances and parties.

Rather than a boat, Margaret and her parents took the deluxe White Train from Cairo down to Assouan, where they stayed at the Cataract Hotel, populated largely by invalids and where a speciality cure for rheumatism involved being buried up to the neck in hot sand. Margaret meanwhile, spent her time exploring on a camel, alone 'except for one Egyptian bodyguard', visiting the Temple of Philae, a number of Coptic churches and going for picnics with the young officers stationed in Cairo who came down to Assouan to spend the weekend. Among these was the handsome Fulke, Earl of Warwick, who was serving with

Sells

◀ Exquisite
advertisement for the
Egypt Travel Bureau
by Gladys Peto, *The
Graphic*, 1930, featuring
tourists in Peto's
trademark colourful
frocks among ancient
ruins. (© Illustrated
London News/
Mary Evans)

▶ According to *The
Traveller* magazine,
advising on what to wear
in Egypt, 'the details
of dress may be the
smartest of those fit
for the London Season'.
Fashion illustration
from French women's
magazine *Femina*,
December 1929,
showing Paul Poiret
fashions in the winter
sun of Heliopolis. (Mary
Evans Picture Library)

PAUL POIRET   PAUL POIRET

◄ Striking Cunard poster advertising cruises to Egypt in the 1930s. (Onslow Auctions Limited/Mary Evans)

▶ 'The Pyramids rise behind and above it; they actually seem in the background of the hotel.' A unique view of the Cheops pyramid from the Mena House Hotel. Opened in 1869, the hotel had previously been a royal hunting lodge. (Grenville Collins Postcard Collection/ Mary Evans)

▶ Cabaret and dancing at the Kit-Kat Club at the Gezirah Palace Hotel, Cairo, in 1930. Agatha Christie had stayed at the hotel as a young debutante, often attending as many as five dances a week. (© Illustrated London News/Mary Evans)

the 1st Battalion, Grenadier Guards in Egypt. In what she described as 'this Arabian Nights atmosphere', Fulke fell hopelessly in love with her and eventually proposed on New Year's Eve. The proposal was accepted, the engagement was announced, the wedding dress ordered and preparations were made for Margaret to become chatelaine of Warwick Castle. But, away from the carefree, moonlit romance of Egypt, Margaret found herself getting cold feet and, just weeks before the wedding, she called it off. It is not unusual for a holiday romance to lose its shine, but in Margaret's case, her change of heart was a very public one. Fulke Warwick was only temporarily disconcerted by Margaret's change of heart. Both of them appear elsewhere in this book, having eventually found love elsewhere.

▲ Evocative poster by Georges Dorival for the new Heliopolis Palace Hotel in Cairo, which opened in December 1910. Boasting 400 bedrooms and an opulent interior, its inaugural ball attracted all of Cairo society. (Cairo Heliopolis Palace Hotel, 1910, Géo Dorival, Atelier Dorival, Paris, 154 x 104cm, Collection Alessandro Bellenda)

'The Man Who Slept Through', by H.M. Bateman, *The Tatler*, 3 June 1951. A spectacular Nile sunset was not to be missed, so a blissfully snoozing passenger is enough to send crew and fellow tourists into paroxysms of consternation in this keenly observed Bateman cartoon. (© Estate of H.M. Bateman/ILN/Mary Evans)

In January 1952, anti-British riots broke out in Cairo following the killing by British occupation troops of fifty Egyptian auxiliary policemen in the city of Ismailia in the Suez zone. Widespread looting and arson took place across the city. Twenty-six people died and among the buildings torched and ruined were Cairo's opera house and the iconic Shepheard's Hotel, once the glamorous centre of Cairo society. Four years later, a coup by the Free Officers Movement of Egypt sought to overthrow King Farouk of Egypt, establish a republic and end British occupation. Two years after that, the Anglo-Egyptian Evacuation Agreement was signed with the final British soldier departing Egypt in June 1956. The Egyptians had finally reclaimed their country, their identity – and their tourist industry – from the British.

7

ST MORITZ

EUROPE'S WINTER PLAYGROUND

IN 1894, SIR ARTHUR CONAN DOYLE was staying with his wife at the Swiss health resort of Davos in a bid to cure her consumptive state of health. During the trip, he became an unlikely pioneer and exponent of the sport of skiing and decided to attempt a trek of 15 miles on skis from Davos to Arosa. Although he embarked on the expedition in the company of two local guides, the Branger brothers, it was still an impressive feat as the route was not for the faint-hearted due to numerous steep inclines. After successfully completing the trek in a time that surprised the bemused Swiss locals, he wrote with exhilaration (and perhaps some exaggeration) of his experiences in *The Strand* – the same magazine that published his famous Sherlock Holmes stories. Conan Doyle was such a convert to this novel method of locomotion that he became evangelical and made an audacious prediction:

> I am convinced that the time will come when hundreds of Englishmen will come to Switzerland for the 'ski-ing' season in March and April I believe that I may claim to be the first save only for two Switzers to do any mountain work (though on a modest enough scale) on snow shoes, but I am certain that I will not by many a thousand be the last.

In November 1900, *The Traveller* magazine ran a feature, with photographs, elaborating on 'the new Alpine winter sport', crediting Conan Doyle with sowing

Front cover of *The Bystander Winter Sports Number* by Bruce Angrave, 5 November 1930. (© Illustrated London News/ Mary Evans)

the seeds for the 'now universal success' of skiing, which it described as 'a cross between skating and tobogganing', and warning that 'the secret of success in skiing down a hill is to keep the feet exactly parallel. Great is the fall of him who neglects this rule.'

By 1907, *The Bystander* was declaring the Swiss winter resorts 'the playground of Europe', with St Moritz itself, situated in the Engadine, arguably Switzerland's most scenic valley, frequently dubbed the 'Paris' or 'Mayfair' of the Alps. In that year, of the 1,800 visitors to St Moritz, nearly half were British. Through the next three decades, St Moritz was to become the unrivalled centre for royalty, aristocracy and celebrities to congregate for a winter sports holiday that was as essential to their social year as a late summer spell at the Venice Lido or an Easter break at Deauville. In 1930, *The Illustrated Sporting and Dramatic News* reported, 'all the Swiss centres confirm that the Alps in January are by no means losing their popularity with attendance higher than ever.' Arthur Conan Doyle would have been delighted that his prediction had proved so accurate.

Skiing was a novelty, but Switzerland's development as a tourist destination had evolved well before its introduction. As with all resorts, the arrival of the railway was a key factor in boosting Switzerland's tourist industry, and its first visitors came, not in the winter, but during the summer instead. There were the inevitable invalids, arriving in the hope that the crystal-clear air and efficient Swiss sanatoriums would prove restorative and send them home cured. But there were holidaymakers too, who came to enjoy bracing walks or to climb mountains, all in a picture-postcard landscape, or perhaps to delight in the Alpine flora and bring home a cuckoo clock as a souvenir. Johannes Badrutt, the owner of the Hotel Kulm at St Moritz, made a bet with his English guests; he promised they would enjoy his sun terrace just as much in the winter months and gave them the guarantee that if they chose to find out, and a winter holiday was not to their taste, then he would refund the cost of their trip. His English visitors did return, and they lingered until spring. St Moritz's winter season was born.

In the 1880s, a Norwegian, Herr Eger, had arrived in Switzerland with a pair of Norwegian skis and introduced a mode of transport completely new to the Swiss, though not to the Germans or Austrians. Even in Britain, north-east miners in the Yorkshire and Durham dales used them in winter and there is mention of skiing in *Lorna Doone*, set in the seventeenth century. The English upper class, with an enthusiasm for all kinds of sport, the more daring the better, began to show an active interest in the potential of winter sport and particularly skiing. Skating, already popular, found an ideal base at St Moritz and the first European

◀ 'You can have a lovely time in being thoroughly lazy.' St Moritz's success had been founded on a wager. Johannes Badrutt, the owner of the Hotel Kulm, had made a bet with his English guests that they would enjoy his sun terrace just as much in the winter months. Illustration by Fortunino Matania in *The Sphere*, 14 February 1914. (© Illustrated London News/ Mary Evans)

Exclusive Bystander Photograph   *By Scaioni Paris.*

Ice Skating Championships were held there in 1882. And while the origins of European skiing lie very much in Norway, it was the British, including Conan Doyle, who were instrumental in establishing Switzerland – and St Moritz – as a premier skiing destination.

Colonel Edward 'Teddy' Richardson, known as 'the father of English skiing', learnt to ski in Norway and in 1890 travelled to Switzerland to introduce the sport. He set up the Davos English Ski Club and was a founder member of the Ski Club of Great Britain, which held its inaugural dinner at the Café Royal in London on 6 May 1903. In that year, Richardson also co-wrote and edited one of the first books on skiing: *Ski Running*. It is significant that within two years, the book's popularity necessitated a second edition.

Sir Henry Lunn, another upper-class British enthusiast, formed the Public Schools Alpine Sports Club in 1905 and persuaded local hotels to cater specifically for the winter sports crowd through his company, Lunn's Travel Agency (later known as Lunn Poly). Sir Henry was the progenitor of a skiing dynasty. His son Arnold invented the slalom ski race and wrote widely on the sport. In an article in *The Graphic* in 1930, he suggested that skiers who cut down their usual ration of cocktails and cigarettes would feel the benefit greatly – a hint no doubt at the preoccupations of most of St Moritz's visitors! Arnold's wife Mabel was the first woman to pass the British First Class skiing test and their son Peter, who was first introduced to skiing just before his second birthday in 1916, went on to compete for Britain in the 1936 Winter Olympics.

Switzerland continued to be a popular summer destination for Thomas Cook tourists, but the winter season was the preserve of the wealthy visitors who descended on Davos, Wengen, Mürren, Zermatt and particularly St Moritz between December and March. They came for a holiday that combined the very highest standard of hospitality and entertainment with strenuous and occasionally death-defying exercise. Between 1897 and 1919, 121 skiers were killed in Switzerland – a statistic that only served to lace a winter holiday with a frisson of excitement.

Even more sedate pursuits came with risks. In 1937, Charles Vivian Jackson was killed while driving a horse-drawn sleigh. His twin brother Derek received the news of his brother's death just as he was embarking on a honeymoon in Vienna following his marriage to Pamela Mitford, the second of the famous Mitford sisters. Citing others who had suffered injuries in similar accidents, *The Bystander* blamed the introduction of motor traffic to the Engadine several years earlier. Elsewhere, horse races took place on the frozen Great Lake, as did ski-joring – a kind of snowy version of water-skiing where skiers travelled at speed behind galloping horses. Winter sports came with associated risks and perhaps most risky of all was St Moritz's infamous Cresta Run.

A winding ice track of three-quarter of a mile, the Cresta, built in 1884, was a magnet for thrill-seeking tobogganists (competitors today must sign a disclaimer before taking part). Reginald Arkell, writing in *The Bystander* in 1927, commented that the Cresta was 'where men who are really men negotiate Sunny Corner' and amateur enthusiasts frequently suffered injury. In 1935, *The Bystander* reported on Lord Hindlip and Ralph Harbord, who had been lucky to escape with a grazed leg and forehead, and a broken shoulder respectively after their 'bob' crash.

The Cresta was one of the highlights of a St Moritz holiday. 'One of the really worthwhile things to do was to watch the Cresta boys', wrote *The Bystander* in 1937, noting, 'the amazingly fresh complexions and starry eyes owned by the Cresta girl-fans who watch these early-morning exploits'. Among the spectators was Lady Warwick, the former Rose Bingham – a beauty whose debut in 1931 had caused quite a stir. Her attempts to film the Cresta riders as they sped past were the subject of much amusement and it is likely that among those daredevil

WINTER SPORT in SWITZERLAND

Special supplement to "The Sphere" depicting Life
and Sport in "The Winter Playground of Europe"

BURBERRY WINTER SPORTS DRESS

supplies the most comfortable and protective equipment for Ski-ing, Skating and Luge-ing.

Designed by experts with an intimate knowledge of the requirements, Burberry models embody all the latest tips, as well as every quality essential to the enjoyment of sport on snow or ice.

Burberry materials, especially woven and proofed for Winter Sports, keep out snow, wind, cold and wet.

They maintain healthful warmth, yet ventilate naturally; are extremely light, yet exceedingly strong; and have finished surfaces to which snow cannot cling.

Catalogue, illustrating new models in colour, and patterns of materials, post free on mention of " The Sphere."

BURBERRYS LTD. HAYMARKET LONDON S.W. I

riders was Billy Fiske. William Meade Lindsay Fiske III, one of the Cresta's most celebrated champions was the Cambridge-educated son of a wealthy American banker. Billy won a gold medal aged just 16 at the 1928 St Moritz Winter Olympic Games as part of the five-man US bobsleigh team, and scooped a second gold in 1932 at Lake Placid. He declined to take part in the 1936 Winter Olympics, disapproving of the Nazi persecution of Jews. Addicted to speed, Billy was also notorious behind the wheel, driving his 4-litre open-top Bentley at breakneck speeds around the country roads of East Anglia during his time at Cambridge, and setting unofficial speed records all over Europe.

Romance blossomed on the slopes of St Moritz after Billy had been introduced to Rose by the actor David Niven. In August 1938, Rose, by now divorced from her husband, married Billy in fashionable Maidenhead, but their marriage was to be tragically short-lived. When war broke out, Billy presented Canadian papers in order to join the RAF as part of the 601 squadron, known as the 'Millionaire's Mob', where the natural reflexes that had made him such a successful bobsleigh rider also made him an instinctive and fearless pilot. The squadron's leader, Archibald Hope, said of him, 'Unquestionably, Billy Fiske was the best pilot I've ever known. It was unbelievable how good he was. He picked it up so fast it wasn't true.' Billy died of shock in August 1940 after piloting his burning Hurricane back to the squadron's airfield, becoming the first US airman to give his life during the Second World War.

Sport was one reason St Moritz drew its high-class crowd, but its après-ski offer was sufficiently sophisticated to lure anyone who lacked the inclination to do anything energetic. 'You can have a lovely time in being thoroughly lazy we found out', noted *The Bystander* in January 1937. Mornings could begin with a glass of 'delicious, hot glühwein on the sun-baked terrace of the Palace Hotel' and afterwards the Corviglia Club beckoned. Accessible by a funicular railway, St Moritz's terribly exclusive mountain club was founded by a group of well-heeled friends, among them Coco Chanel and Jacques Cartier, to provide a place to congregate between skiing bouts. It once famously refused access to Eleanor Roosevelt, the doormen deciding she looked too dowdy to be a VIP. The Corviglia's terrace was lined with long trestle tables where guests could enjoy hot soup for lunch, a cocktail or two, and then snooze in the sun. Evenings at the club were illuminated by candles in bottles and, afterwards, intrepid types could ski back to their hotels, their route downhill lit only by stars and guides with torches.

The Palace Hotel, looking over the village's lake, was the centre of social life in St Moritz, with a large restaurant and a special supper room, The

◄ Burberry
advertisement, by
Fortunino Matania, 1928,
offering smart ski-wear
for the discerning
British holidaymaker.
© Illustrated London
News/Mary Evans)

Embassy, where dancing took place nightly. Opened by Caspar Badrutt (the son of Johannes Badrutt) in 1896, with its turrets and terraces looking over the lake, the hotel's fairy-tale appearance reflected its regal name. At the Palace, high japes were the order of the day. In 1937, a mock Cresta Run at the Curzon Cup Ball wreaked as much havoc as the real-life version. *The Bystander* reported:

◀ Even the dogs were stylish on the slopes of St Moritz. The American actress Melitta Mara with her dog Frisco in 1939. (Imagno/ Mary Evans)

> It was a small wooden chute with a couple of bends, and you went down (if you were lucky) on a cushion, but such was the hurry and impatience of the ever-waiting queue that you probably slid down on your very best dress and got a splinter or two into the bargain. Miss Desiree de la Tour did considerable damage to a lovely white dress; Lady Plunket's pale blue sequins were torn off by the yard; Lady Moira Forbes hurt her wrist.

◀ Miss Margaret Whigham, later Mrs Charles Sweeny and then the infamous Duchess of Argyll whose 1963 divorce case scandalised the country, pictured at St Moritz with the Marquess of Donegall (Edward Chichester) in 1930 – the year she was presented at court. The 6th Marquess was a journalist and staff writer for the *Daily Sketch*, covering winter sports in St Moritz. (© Illustrated London News/Mary Evans)

▶ 'The Ski Forest', by Fleming Williams, *The Illustrated Sporting and Dramatic News*, 15 January 1927. A typical scene at midday at the top of any well-known ski climb, with as many as 100 skis standing up in the snow to dry while their owners rest and lunch at the 'hut'. (© Illustrated London News/ Mary Evans)

Those damaged evening frocks would not have been cheap. Fashion and style were just as important in St Moritz as anywhere, although women often remained in their trousers or plus-fours and sweaters for the pre-prandial cocktail, before finally getting changed for dinner. Ski-wear became a new area for the Parisian couture houses to explore. Both Elsa Schiaparelli and Jean Patou designed ski-wear collections for the winter seasons of the inter-war years, and the British company Burberry engaged the services of the artist Fortunino Matania to illustrate their advertisements with scenes of fashionable society in the snow. As their owners turned the ski slopes into a fashion runway, even pets got in on the act. Mrs Jack Heaton was at St Moritz in 1938 with her poodle who wore specially made leather laced boots – the latest doggy fashion to protect paws from the icy conditions. Dressing up was all part of the scene, and particularly popular were daytime ice carnivals and evening fancy-dress galas. Skaters dressed in an array of costumes from Victorian crinolines to pantomime horses created a peculiar spectacle on St Moritz's ice rinks, and made perfect picture stories for the press.

As an only child of wealthy parents, Margaret Whigham was a veteran of holidays spent in some of the world's most prestigious resorts. She visited

◀ Spanish tennis player Lilí Álvarez performing a very passable ski jump at St Moritz in 1927. Although best known as a tennis player – she was ranked in the top ten during the late 1920s and early 1930s – she was a sporting all-rounder and, having been brought up in Switzerland, was a skilled ice skater and alpine skier.
(© Illustrated London News/Mary Evans)

▼ Ice carnival at St Moritz, 1927. Fancy dress on skates was one of the novelties of a holiday at the resort.
(© Illustrated London News/Mary Evans)

'The Man Who Threw
Snowball at St Moritz',
y H.M. Bateman, *The
atler*, 26 November
926. Bateman's 'Man
Vho' cartoons in *The
atler* poked fun at the
agazine's readership
nd brilliantly captured
e withering effects of
n ill-timed social faux
as.(© Estate of H.M.
ateman/ILN/
1ary Evans)

St Moritz each winter with her parents after they had moved to England in the late 1920s. Keen to shield their young daughter from the worldlier atmosphere of the Palace, for the first two years they stayed at the family-friendly Suvretta Hotel, which was half an hour away. Much to Margaret's delight, for their third holiday her parents chose the Palace, where she immensely enjoyed dancing the tango with the wealthy and handsome Argentines who frequented St Moritz at that time. She was taught to ski by a number of willing volunteers including familiar St Moritz visitors Bobbie Cunningham-Reid, the dashing husband of Mary Ashley who was the sister of Edwina Mountbatten and the Marquess of Donegall. In January 1930, she was pictured in *The Sketch* with the latter, who had been educated partly in Switzerland and, in his role as a journalist for the *Daily Sketch*, regularly reported on the gossip from St Moritz.

PRINTED IN SWITZERLAND

◀ A bold and optimistic poster by Alois Carigiet from 1934 summing up the playful atmosphere of St Moritz. (St Moritz, 1932, Alois Carigiet, 65 x 101.7cm, Wolfsberg, Zürich, Galleria L'IMAGE, Alassio)

Other regulars at the Mayfair of Engadine included the glamorous entertainers the Dolly Sisters; tennis stars Lilí Álvarez (a very competent skier) and Suzanne Lenglen; Clementine Churchill; and Barbara Hutton, who announced her engagement to the fourth of her seven husbands at St Moritz. Charles Laughton once presided over the Palace Hotel's children's Christmas party, champion jockey Gordon Richards won a fancy-dress gala at St Moritz in 1927 dressed as a diminutive sailor and in 1928 two of Britain's hottest writers, Michael Arlen and Noël Coward, were pictured in the papers larking about on a sledge. Lady Diana Cooper was regularly in charge of the cabaret entertainments at the Carlton Hotel, which opened in 1913 and was where the exiled King Constantine of Greece and his children spent much of the First World War. There were, of course, certain figures who were permanent fixtures at the resort, from the Eton-educated Spanish diplomat the Duke of Alba, who was instrumental in founding the Corviglia Skiing Club, to Lady Deterding, the Russian wife of Sir Henri, chairman of the Royal Dutch Petroleum Company, whose lavish lunch parties gathered together the cream of St Moritz society. Also notable was Francis Curzon, brother of Lord Curzon, the Viceroy of India and founder of the St Moritz Tobogganing Club, who 'created the winter sports at St. Moritz', according to *The Bystander* in its 1933 review of the resort's prominent figures. 'His interest goes back twenty-five years at least, and he has always been a pillar to the sports clubs there of every kind,' it added.

St Moritz remains the gold standard for winter holidays and its so-called 'champagne climate' continues to give it the edge over rival resorts. The tanned skiers populating its slopes today may be more likely to be drawn from the international jet set, but its fame and fortune owe much to one enterprising Swiss hotel owner and a band of intrepid, sports-loving Britons.

HARROGATE

Free Brochure, etc., from F. J. C. BROOME
HARROGATE

8

ENGLAND

SPAS AND SEASIDE, RIVERSIDE CLUBS AND ROADHOUSES

IN 1926, HARROGATE, North Yorkshire's elegant and respectable spa town, was in the news. Agatha Christie, the crime novelist, had unexpectedly disappeared from her Berkshire home triggering a frantic, nationwide search. While the police dredged the ominously named Silent Pool, Albury, near to where her car had been found abandoned, and the newspapers were feverishly speculating on her whereabouts, Christie had taken the train to Harrogate where she took a room on the first floor of the ivy-clad Hydro Hotel. She gave her name as Mrs Teresa Neele of Cape Town. Towards the end of her week-and-a-half stay in Harrogate, some of the staff began to suspect that the mysterious Mrs Neele may in fact be the Mrs Christie, whose photograph had been splashed all over the tabloid newspapers. Most remained silent on the subject: Harrogate was a discreet place. The privacy and comfort of the guests were a priority.

During her stay, Christie took her meals in the Hydro Hotel's dining room and afterwards would read or enjoy the band playing in the Winter Garden Ballroom. On a couple of occasions, she sang to a piano accompaniment. She joined the W.H. Smith Library, indulged in some spa treatments at the hotel and had a Turkish bath at the Royal Spa. She is likely to have walked around the Valley Gardens with its new cloister-like sun walk, listened to a morning concert at the Royal Baths Gardens or tasted the sulphurous waters at one of the pump rooms. Having arrived at Harrogate with the clothes she stood up in, she also

◀ 1920s poster promoting Harrogate, by Reginald Higgins. Higgins designed a number of travel posters, and was renowned for depicting the 'modern girl' in many of his magazine illustrations. His bold, flat poster style and the chic women helped to position Harrogate as the stylish destination it aspired to be. (Mary Evans Picture Library)

HOT AIR TREATMENT (ORVILLE SYSTEM) ROYAL BATHS HARROGATE.

frequented the smart shops in Harrogate's centre where she bought dresses, hats and twin sets.

Decades of theorists have deliberated over Agatha Christie's state of mind during her eleven-day disappearance, but her behaviour in Harrogate was unremarkable. Such activities were typical of the Harrogate visitor. And Harrogate was a typical destination for an upper-middle-class woman like Agatha Christie. The ensueing sensationalism of the search for her entirely ignored the fact that she had written to her brother-in-law to say she was going to stay at a Yorkshire spa. It didn't take Hercule Poirot to detect where she might be, and yet her whereabouts were eventually discovered when two members of the Hydro Hotel's orchestra went to the police with their suspicions.

Harrogate's status as a spa town dates back to the beginning of the seventeenth century when a well-travelled local, Captain William Slingsby, likened Harrogate's waters to those taken for medicinal purposes at spas on the Continent. In 1842, the Royal Pump Room was built over the old sulphur well, as more hotels were built to accommodate the visitors who flocked to the town to

▲ A remarkable array of paraphernalia in the hot-air treatment room of the Royal Baths at Harrogate. Despite its long-held reputation as a spa town, Harrogate was aware it needed to keep pace with rival resorts in Europe and continued to offer a wide range of treatments and cures. (Grenville Collins Postcard Collection/ Mary Evans)

take the waters. By the time of the First World War, in direct challenge to spas in Europe, the Royal Baths were offering eighty curative treatments ranging from Nauheim baths for heart problems and Aix and Vichy douches to Ems inhalation rooms and an extensive Plombière installation for colitis. All this and without the ordeal of travelling to the Continent when in poor health, especially when, in 1921, the London North Eastern Railway (LNER) established a Pullman rail service direct to Harrogate from King's Cross.

In addition, the Corporation of Harrogate, which owned the Bath and the Royal Halls, co-ordinated with the town's big hotels and boarding houses to ensure a constant programme of comforts and entertainment for visitors. It even employed a Director of Music, Julian Clifford, who ensured a daily programme of music could be had in various venues around the town, from as early as 7.30 a.m. at the Royal Pump Room. Magazines reported on Harrogate's 'Season' as the autumn months, though in truth the town attracted visitors all year round. Nevertheless, one report on Harrogate's season in September 1933 pictured Sir Woodman Burbidge, the owner of Harrods, with his family outside the Majestic Hotel. The previous year, *The Bystander* published a photograph of Lady Wood, the wife of the Conservative politician and Postmaster General Sir Kingsley Wood, trying to give a sporting smile for the cameras after taking a swig of the famous waters.

Comfortable, dependable and seamlessly organised, Harrogate was also blessed with myriad sightseeing opportunities within easy reach by car, from the scenic Yorkshire Dales to grand stately homes such as Harewood House. But its inherent qualities also meant it lacked the racy sophistication of French continental resorts – a fact William Comyns Beaumont, editor of *The Bystander* magazine, was quick to point out when he motored up there in a black six-cylinder Stutz saloon in 1926 (the same year of Agatha Christie's retreat). He was dismayed to find a 'depressing atmosphere of Victorianism'. 'Everyone is deemed to be an invalid or semi-invalid, and an intolerably dull atmosphere is created. If one is in rude health one feels more than half ashamed of the fact. Ten o'clock is the average bed-time.' The Corporation, no doubt aware of such opinions, and not wishing to alienate Harrogate's traditional clientele, promoted the town as the best of both worlds. 'The Mecca of the Ailing; The Playground of the Robust', proclaimed a 1928 advertisement, which added, 'All that is best in English Old World associations and exquisite scenery, coupled with present-day fashion and smartness, is epitomised at Harrogate'.

For Agatha Christie, Harrogate offered her exactly what she needed. Her marriage to her first husband Archie was in difficulties. The couple had grown

apart and Archie was involved with another woman; her escape to Yorkshire was an attempt to shock him into realising what he might lose. But the town, with its solid stone buildings, its kindly but efficient people and its pleasant diversions, could make anyone feel safe and cared for. Harrogate also bore similarities to a place she had been particularly happy – Torquay, where she had been born and brought up.

As with Harrogate, and a number of south coast resorts, Torquay's success was attributed to invalids who came principally for its exceptionally mild winter climate. It was also impossibly pretty, causing even Napoleon, who spotted it while a prisoner on the *Bellerophon*, to exclaim, 'How beautiful! I should like to live there.' It found popularity with the Russian aristocracy, particularly Grand Duchess Marie, elder sister of Tsar Alexander II, and at one time or another it hosted Benjamin Disraeli, Elizabeth Barrett Browning and the wealthy philanthropist Baroness Angela Burdett-Coutts. Tennyson, who visited Torquay early in its development as a seaside resort, declared it 'the loveliest sea-village in England'. In 1886, following a mild case of diphtheria, Alexandra, Princess of Wales, stayed at the resort with her daughters.

Torquay was a serene place; its elegant buildings nestled snugly and sympathetically among the undulations of its seven hills. It was a town where people came to be cared for and to regain their health. Lovely it may have been, but its staid reputation prompted even Rudyard Kipling to write, 'Torquay is such a place as I do desire to upset by dancing through it with nothing on but my spectacles.' While not exactly suffering from an image problem, the increase in foreign travel meant Torquay began to lose its quality visitors to more exotic destinations. Action was required to save its status as one of the UK's most distinguished seaside resorts.

In the early 1920s, the Great Western Railway (GWR) began to heavily promote its service to the West Country on the Torbay Express, which left Paddington daily at noon and transported passengers to the Devon coast in just three and a half hours. Supplementing this were numerous magazine advertorials heaping praise on Torquay's world-class climate, delightful scenery and peerless amusements. The medical baths were given a complete overhaul in 1922 at a cost of £25,000, opening as the Marine Spa with a new Vita-glass sun lounge with sea view and spa treatments including Torbay seaweed baths and Dartmoor peat packs. The focus now was on 'wellness' rather than 'cure' as, just like Harrogate, Torquay sought to lure the young and healthy as well as the infirm.

Glamorous Torquay, as imagined by William . Sennett on the front cover of a resort brochure from around 1925. (Mary Evans Picture Library)

A new road, the Marine Drive, was built, allowing motorists access to some of the bay's most attractive coves and vistas. Scientific recordings of the town's sunshine proved it could hold its own with an average winter temperature of 46.9°F (8.3°C), 'practically the same as that of Nice'. 'There are few sunless days during the winter months,' claimed *The Sphere*, 'and in every respect, Torquay is a superior alternative to the much-boomed Continental resorts.' The town was also given a confident, almost audacious strapline: Queen of the English Riviera. The branding was a warning shot to the places that had dared to poach Torquay's high-class customers. *The Sphere* magazine in 1929 argued the case for Torquay:

> What Monte Carlo is to the French Riviera that Torquay is to the Riviera of England. Overhead is the same blue sky and the same bright sun, and at its feet is the sea of the same deep blue as the Mediterranean, while palms and other sub-tropical flowers and plants flourish in the open just as they do in the popular French resort.

Comparisons with the French Riviera were more than PR puff. With its southern aspect, villas built on slopes overlooking the hills and its palm trees, Torquay felt like a very English version of a town on the Côte d'Azur. Many French resorts had, of course, grown as a refuge for invalids too, and, just like Cannes and Monte Carlo, Torquay had gained the patronage of wealthy Russian visitors during the nineteenth century. What it needed to do in the aftermath of the First World War – a time when new resorts were appearing in southern France and old ones were reinventing themselves – was find ways to appeal to an increasingly discerning customer.

Torquay's hotels joined in this general spruce up. The Imperial Hotel, where Napoleon III had once enjoyed a restorative break, styled itself 'an English hotel in the Mediterranean manner' in its advertisements. In the 1930s, the bar at the Grand Hotel was considered fashionable enough to feature in a series of advertisements for Booth's Gin. The Osborne Hotel, set in a sylvan location on the slopes of Lincombe Woods at the start of the much-lauded Marine Drive, made much of the fact that all of its 150 rooms came with hot and cold running water. The hotel had a fine selection of hard and grass tennis courts, and milk for guests came from its own herd of tuberculin-tested Guernsey cows. Most modern and, as its name suggested, palatial, was the Palace Hotel, which opened in August 1921. Originally an Italianate villa, it was extended to provide 141 rooms.

◀ A 1929 sketch by *The Bystander* magazine's artist, Helen McKie, in the grounds of the Palace Hotel in Torquay, where the terrors of an English autumn and winter hold no sway ... where the soft breezes and warm sunshine make this part of South Devon one of the most favoured spots in the British Isles'. Extended from a Victorian Italianate villa, the 141-room hotel opened in 1921 offering every modern amenity to the discerning visitor. It closed in 2017. (© Illustrated London News/Mary Evans)

◄ Bathing cove at Torquay in the 1870s with a neat row of bathing huts. The beautiful Devon coastlir and mild microclimate first attracted visitors t the town. Napoleon had even expressed a desire to live there when he spotted it as a prisoner on the *Bellerophon* in 1815. (Mary Evans Picture Library)

The hotel once played host to rising British tennis players Angela Mortimer and Sue Barker, both of whom were coached at the Palace's tennis courts. But in 2017, the hotel closed; its inability to fill rooms and remain a sustainable business was an acute reflection of Torquay's decline from the flourishing and fashionable resort it once was.

The Essex coastal town of Frinton-on-Sea seems an unlikely location for the cream of society, but in the first half of the twentieth century, it too was one of the most popular, and exclusive, resorts. The town was founded by Sir Richard Powell Cooper, a businessman from Lichfield whose fortune came from a family business specialising in agricultural and veterinary products, particularly several highly effective forms of sheep dip. Cooper purchased land at the small settlement of Frinton in 1893 with the intention of creating 'a high class and select watering hole'. His vision for Frinton was a wholesome, genteel and restrained coastal retreat – everything the typical seaside town was not. He created a golf course first (naturally) and proceeded to sell off large plots of land where substantial houses in the Tudorbethan, baronial and Arts and Crafts styles were built along wide, tree-lined avenues. One house, The Homestead, was designed by Charles Voysey and survives today as one of the finest examples of his architecture. Later, between 1934 and 1936, the architect Oliver Hill, a disciple of the Modern Movement, began to build an estate of art deco houses at Frinton after being inspired by the modernist villas he had seen on the French Riviera. The scheme soon ran out of investment, but the forty buildings that remain are a surprising modernist experiment in the midst of an essentially conservative town.

Writing in *The Sketch* in 1932, Pamela Murray wondered why Frinton didn't just 'abolish the sea altogether, or cover it with a tarpaulin a la Centre Court, so that nobody could possibly confuse Frinton with one of those AWFUL seaside places where concert parties and weighing machines adorn the "prom"'. But this was Frinton's unique character. Cycling was banned along the seafront and even the famous Frinton gates at the level crossing symbolically divided the town's most exclusive streets from the less salubrious developments beyond. There was no pier, unlike Walton-on-the-Naze 1½ miles along the coast. There were no pubs, no amusement arcades and no ice cream or whelk sellers plying their wares. All of which also meant: no riff-raff.

The most successful British resorts, such as Margate and Blackpool, had grown rapidly due to the railways bringing working-class visitors from big cities, each vying with the other to lure visitors with a pungent mix of a fairground and pier amusements, dance halls, fish and chips, and souvenir shops. In contrast, Frinton-on-Sea, through a variety of by-laws and legal covenants, created a pleasant but sanitised refuge free from the rowdy vulgarity of the more popular seaside haunts. Smart beach huts lined the sandy beach and, above that, the neatly manicured 'greensward' – a stretch of grass over a mile in length – divided it from the esplanade in place of the usual promenade. Other than municipal flower troughs and a few benches and shelters available to take in the unremarkable view of the North Sea, the greensward remains today as it was at the beginning of the twentieth century. There were no betting shops and absolutely no public houses – Frinton's visitors enjoyed a tipple in hotel restaurants or club bars so surely there was no need! It was a conscious decision on the part of Frinton's town fathers to discourage the wrong sort and reassure the type of visitors they hoped to attract. *The Bystander* magazine,

which had a maverick tendency to lightly mock the very people it reported on, published a poem about Frinton in 1933 under the title 'Popular Playgrounds', with one verse summing up its exclusive pretensions:

> No motor coaches may set down
> Within this most exclusive town
> Their loads of vulgar trippers who
> Would rollick by the billows blue,
> For Frinton frowns severely at
> The plaguey proletariat,
> Discouraging that jocund joy
> So oft evinced by hoi polloi;
> So public bars with bitter beer
> Are NOT in evidence down here!

Frinton finally got its first and, so far, only pub in 2000. The town's main shopping thoroughfare, Connaught Avenue, was known as the 'Bond Street of East Anglia', a name it still rather optimistically hangs on to despite the inevitable appearance of numerous charity shops. It remains pleasingly eclectic, however, and vestiges of its smarter former self remain in the form of some original shop-front features and stained-glass windows.

Free of the sights of carousing couples, drunken crowds or unwholesome arcades, and with its clean, sandy beach and proximity to London, Frinton was the natural choice for society parents to bring their children for a holiday. Each summer, magazines like *The Sketch* and *The Tatler* would feature 'well-knowns' at Frinton: perhaps Gladys Cooper on the beach with her children John and Joan; Princess Otto von Bismarck; or the Hon. Mrs Ian Campbell, daughter of Lord Beaverbrook, paddling in the sea with little Jeanne Louise. Pamela Murray confirmed that Frinton was where 'all the very best children dig attended by pyjama-clad parents who have brought their camel coats in case the climate goes bad on them'. Elsewhere, the Frinton Lawn Tennis tournament attracted some of the game's leading players. Its well-attended junior tournament was of particular interest and considered a hotbed for rising talent, with players like a young Eileen Bennett regularly competing. In 1922, Winston Churchill's children, Randolph and Diana, took part in the junior mixed doubles, while speculation was rife as to whether Graham Chambers, son of the Wimbledon champion Dorothea Lambert Chambers, would have inherited his mother's ruthless on-court technique.

◄ Poster promoting Torquay, by William A. Bennett, 1929. There was heavy investment in promoting the West Country as a holiday destination in the 1920s. Torquay, 1929, William A. Sennett, J. Weiner Ltd, London, 126.8 x 102cm, Galleria L'IMAGE, Alassio)

◄ In the decade leading up to the First World War, Dorothea Douglass Lambert Chambers was the outstanding female tennis player of her generation. She won the Wimbledon singles championship seven times and scooped a gold medal at the 1908 Olympics. Frinton regularly held a well-attended tennis tournament for children. Here Mrs Lambert Chambers' younger son, 11-year-old Graham, seems concerned he may not be able to live up to his mother's colossal reputation. (© Illustrated London News/ Mary Evans)

◄ The actress Gladys Cooper with her children Joan and John on the beach at Frinton-on-Sea in 1927. As well as its sandy beach, Frinton's exclusive and unblemished reputation made it the ideal location for the upper classes and celebrities to bring their children for a wholesome family holiday. (© Illustrated London News/ Mary Evans)

In Frinton, Richard Cooper had created his own utopian idyll from scratch, and in appearance and spirit the town has changed relatively little over the years. About halfway along the greensward, a plaque from the year 2000 commemorates his efforts: 'To remember Richard Powell Cooper – his vision and generosity changed a small village into this charming town renowned for its sands, greensward, tree-lined avenues and tranquility.'

Harrogate, Torquay and Frinton each had their unique characters, but were united in their desire to attract a certain class of holidaymaker. But what about people like William Comyns Beaumont, who had found Harrogate so 'intolerably dull'? There was a growing market among the young, metropolitan set for a destination that would satisfy their appetite for cocktails, jazz and dancing, as well as the escalating cult of health, fitness and the body beautiful, typified by the popularity of swimming and sunbathing. Combining all these ingredients would create an exciting but short-lived leisure phenomenon in the inter-war years. 'Those who say England is dull don't know where to look for adventure,' wrote Comyns Beaumont as he introduced a feature entitled 'Our Great Gay Roads' in *The Bystander* in 1933. Springing up along the artery roads leading out of London, as well as in towns along the River Thames, were a number of inns, entertainment complexes and so-called roadhouses, following the formula of the American country club. All of them catered at varying levels to the growing enthusiasm for sport, swimming and sunbathing, offering state-of-the-art facilities in picturesque settings alongside dancing, dining, cabaret and cocktails, often around the clock. Aimed at a wealthy clientele, many of them styled themselves as destinations for the summer months with 'sunbath' terraces, pools and outdoor dance floors.

By the mid 1930s, roadhouses could be found around Britain but the most significant concentration was in the Home Counties in an area close to London and its more affluent, car-owning demographic. Cars were essential for travelling to roadhouses which, as their name suggests, were located beside or close to main roads, many of which – the Great West Road and Kingston Bypass among them – had been built in the 1920s. These suburban temples of leisure and consumption catered to every desire. In our traffic-choked, gridlocked times, a stay in a hotel just minutes from a motorway or A-road is a far cry from our idea of a luxurious mini-break. But in the 1930s, motoring, and the 'romance of the road', was framed as an aspirational pleasure. Speeding out of town, hopefully with a pretty girl for company, was the chic way to spend the weekend, and the roadhouse fulfilled a desire among the

upper-middle classes seeking good times just a short drive from home. Most offered accommodation – or at least the comparative privacy of a car park – and with it the delicious, sinful possibility of illicit sex if a partner was willing. Even for those who didn't own a car, there was always the option of hiring one from a company with a fleet of smart, nippy open tops and saloons. Godfrey Davis of Albemarle Street in Mayfair could deliver and then pick up a motor the following morning at short notice.

The settings and facilities on offer at these venues sound idyllic. Beaumont described Martin's at Wokingham as having 'a dainty and select bathing pool which draws those who know from all quarters. It stands in the midst of a beautiful garden fringed by firs and poplars'. Downs Hotel at Hassocks, about 12 miles outside of Brighton, had an ultra-modern Vita-glass 'Restorium' (a kind of conservatory), as well as a sunbathing deck constructed and decorated to mimic an ocean liner.

On a Saturday night, the renowned Ace of Spades on the Kingston bypass stayed open late, until 3 or 4 a.m., so revellers could trip the light fantastic to Percy Chandler and his band. It also boasted a polo ground and a private landing strip for the minority of guests arriving by aeroplane. And for ladies who wished to swim but remain into the evening to dine and dance, a make-up department was on hand to groom them into elegant perfection. There was a twin Ace of Spades on the Great West Road and both venues emphasised their status as the original roadhouse – a claim given the royal stamp of approval when the Prince of Wales visited one evening. Along with many other roadhouses, the Ace of Spades was not licensed. This meant guests had to bring their own alcohol, but it also meant they were rarely subject to licensing laws or curfews. Certainly, the inability to buy drinks on the premises did the Ace of Spades very little harm, according to *The Bystander*, writing in 1932:

> I went down to the Ace of Spades on the Kingston by-pass the other evening and found the place crowded. It was a cool evening, but the water was so warm that you could see the steam rising and several people stayed in the water for at least half an hour. This roadhouse must be coining money. There is not a table to be had at 10 p.m., or again at 12 p.m. or 2 a.m., which are the three most popular times. The fact that there is no licence means to say that the guests can arrive American-fashion with their own drink – be it champagne, whisky, brandy, or what have you. The management provide the food, cabaret, two dance orchestras, and swimming pool, and you do the rest. Up to 9.20 p.m., they can send out for your liquor locally. After that, as I say, you must bring it yourself.

The popularity of the Ace of Spades spawned similar venues in the years that followed. The Laughing Water, built on the fishponds belonging to the Earl of Darnley at Cobham in Kent, was fashioned to look like a steamship deck, with its view over the water. In Esher, The Gay Adventure Roadhouse was situated conveniently close to the Brooklands Club, had lawns sloping down to the River Mole (a temperature-controlled pool), and was overseen by Mrs Cook, who also ran a restaurant in Soho's Denman Street. Apparently her omelettes were legendary.

The SHOW BOAT

MAIDENHEAD

There are many roadhouses, but only one "Show-boat," and that is at Maidenhead. ● "The Show-boat" is now open. It only remains for you to come to it, to swim in its pool, dive from its boards, sunbathe on its terraces, take refreshments on its tea terraces, dine and dance in its magnificent ultra-modern ballroom. ● "The Show-boat" will be the Mecca of all those people who wish to enjoy the pleasure of happy sunlit hours and jolly evenings in pleasant, restful surroundings. ● To get to "The Show-boat" you go straight down the Great West Road, on, on, till the sign post says: Maidenhead 5 miles. Then cross over the first bridge and take the second turning on the left and there you are.

Others included the Blue Pool at Camberley, the Water Splash at Colney in Hertfordshire, the Anne Boleyn Hotel at Staines Bridge, Morrell's at West Wickham and Welwyn's Clock House. Some were thoroughly modern, while others adapted and made much of a building's heritage. The Hautboy at Ockham had a baronial-style dining room, while at Great Fosters at Egham, once a home of Elizabeth I, waiting staff fully embraced the era in Tudor-style uniforms.

Newly built establishments aimed for excellence through innovation and developments on a grand scale. The Lagoon in Orpington, at 200 x 40ft, was the largest lido pool in south-east England, with a capacity for 1,500 bathers. Opened at the beginning of June 1933, its proprietors planned to build a huge restaurant, a dance hall and twenty tennis courts, and offer unlimited parking. At the Chase in Ingatestone in Essex, a site was laid out over 18 acres; one side of its swimming pool lay along a sunken terrace, allowing diners to view underwater swimmers through the glass.

In 1931, Poulsen's Club opened at Datchet, close to the Denham film studios, most likely by the same Mr Poulsen who ran the Café de Paris in central London. Its launch was attended by some of London's most prominent socialites, including Margaret Whigham, Lady Bridget Poulett and Cecil Beaton's two sisters, Nancy and Baba. The following year, Poulsen's was the finishing point for a famous scavenger hunt. Participants were tasked with picking up objects, including a lock of platinum hair, a baby's bottle and a photograph of Hitler, before dashing to Datchet, where Prince George, the future Duke of Kent, happened to be dining.

The rise of the roadhouse was rapid and in 1932 a stage play of the same name by Walter Hackett turned the concept into a cultural phenomenon. Set at the ancient Angel Inn, modernised to become the Angel Face Roadhouse, the theatrical version was described by *The Guardian*, with tongue in cheek, as the 'most classy of the licensed bathing establishments that ever decorated a by-pass'. Inside the theatre programme were advertisements for Maison Lyons chocolates, illustrated with art deco figures enjoying typical roadhouse pursuits such as tennis and sunbathing, and another publicising the real-life Ace of Spades. *Roadhouse* was made into a film two years later, and the phenomenon was soon picked up by writers, who found it the ideal setting for crime or romance novels – a trend that ultimately would tinge the roadhouse with a disreputable quality.

In their heyday of 1933, when the roadhouse was a byword for glamour and sophistication, newsreels fed the cinema-going public a series of films on 'Outer London Clubs and Cabarets' featuring places like the Hungaria and

◄ Magazine advertisement for the ambitiously modern Show Boat at Maidenhead, built in an art deco style inspired by the ocean liner in the early 1930s at a cost of £21,000. Like other roadhouses and riverside clubs, it offered swimming, sunbathing and sport together with cocktails, dining, dancing and cabaret. Its heyday was short-lived and today it is earmarked for demolition. (© Illustrated London News/ Mary Evans)

At BRAY by the SILVER THAMES

BY HELEN McKIE

When the sultry summer nights make Town seem heavy and oppressive there is no more pleasant place
to spend an evening than by the river. The Hotel de Paris at Bray, with its cool rooms and pretty lawns
with their bright coloured sunshades, shady trees and glass dance floor, forms an ideal setting which is
enhanced by the sight of the river glinting romantically in the moonlight

Ace of Spades. Even if the majority of those watching could not imagine ever frequenting such places, the newsreels nevertheless lodged the racy and sophisticated world of the roadhouse in the public's collective consciousness.

One of the most ambitious launches during this period was the Showboat at Maidenhead. Designed by Eric Norman Bailey and an Indian architect, D.C. Wadhwa, at a cost of £21,000, the Showboat was, like Downs Hotel, inspired by one of art deco's most influential themes: the ocean liner. Lighting was 'suggestive of a steamship' and the sunbathing terraces allowed one to 'relax under Riviera conditions' enjoying a 'cooling drink and a cigarette', according to one advertisement from 1933. Membership to the Showboat Club, on the same site, cost 10 shillings a year and allowed access to the smart cocktail bar overlooking the swimming pool. The Showboat's location – Maidenhead – was already a well-established centre for out-of-town entertainment going back to the nineteenth century. Its attractive position on the River Thames meant that it became a focus for regattas, especially after 1865, when officers of the Brigade of Guards started a summer riverside boat club.

Boat-mad Victorians and Edwardians flocked to Maidenhead to enjoy a leisurely punt on the meandering river at weekends, to dress in the latest summer fashions, to see and be seen, or at least watch from the riverbank. Most famous was Ascot Sunday, when the river at Boulter's Lock became a picturesque jam of boats and passengers. The area's fashionable credentials were further enhanced by the colony of stage stars that bought homes along the Thames with gardens backing on to the river. Among the first was the celebrated actor-manager David Garrick, who purchased Hampton House in 1759. Many others followed suit over the next century and a half. Hoping perhaps for a tranquil retreat at a short distance from the West End theatres, most riverside homeowners had to tolerate the boat companies that ran sightseeing trips where dwellings and gardens belonging to the famous were pointed out to gawping passengers.

One of the landmark venues in Maidenhead was Skindles Hotel. Originally the Orkney Arms, it was opened by William Skindle in 1833, a century before Bright Young Things were swimming lengths in the pool of the sleek and streamlined Showboat. A short and convenient hop by train from Paddington, Skindles positioned itself as a stylish destination for the smart set and was favoured by King Edward VII, who went there to quaff brandy and soda. As befitted a hotel patronised by the country's most prominent adulterer, Skindles also gained a reputation as the place to go for extramarital liaisons; a popular saying

◄ Scenes at the magical Hotel de Paris in Bray, pictured by Helen McKie in *The Bystander*, 1929. A popular nightspot for fun seekers looking to escape London for the evening, on offer were cool rooms, pretty lawns, bright-coloured sunshades, shady trees and a glass dance floor, all by the river 'glinting romantically in the moonlight'. (© Illustrated London News/ Mary Evans)

before the war was 'Are you married or do you live in Maidenhead?' Skindles' sophisticated but saucy character put Maidenhead on the social map, and over the years more restaurants and riverside clubs opened in the area, forming a style of entertainment complex that would be an antecedent of the roadhouse. *The Bystander* explained in August 1932:

> During these hot nights numbers of people are driving down to the river of its vicinity. Barry Neame, who runs the Hind's Head at Bray, has been having a great success with his establishment which, though not a road-house itself, blazed the way for the Ace of Spades and others of that ilk. His visitors' book of the last few weeks bristles with the names of well-knowns like the Milford Havens, the Philip Astleys, Sir Harold Wernher, and so on.

In 1913, Canadian Jack May opened Murray's nightclub in Soho's Beak Street and, two years later, he had extended his empire by opening a summer outpost at Maidenhead, on the other side of the river to Skindles. A venue for fashion shows and theatrical parties, Murray's, with its glass dance floor, was an immediate success, helped no doubt by the attendance at its launch party of the stage's most popular actresses, including Lee White and Phyllis Monkman.

Also in Maidenhead, the Hungaria Club, sister to Joseph Vecchi's landmark restaurant of the same name in central London, promised 'a shady garden with a blue-lined pool with water very pure and fresh'. Like most of these outposts, it was run by a manager (usually Italian) with experience gained at a smart central London restaurant or hotel – in the Hungaria's case, Zapellini, who had previously been at the Piccadilly Grill. The Hungaria's evening entertainment during the 1930s included a dance troupe known as the Lovelier Lovelies, and Douglas Byng, an entertainer whose camp innuendo felt entirely at home among Maidenhead's worldly crowd.

Visitors to nearby Bray could choose fine dining at the Hind's Head (still flourishing today as a Michelin-starred restaurant run by Heston Blumenthal) or visit the elegant Hôtel de Paris, run by Mr Charles, formerly of Claridge's, where, according to Comyns Beaumont, 'velvety lawns kiss the shimmering Thames'. Beaumont's continuing description is both tantalising and transporting: 'There is something sublime, by twilight, to lounge in an easy chair by the river, hear the band play soft music in the distance, watch the lovely girls in thin, summer frocks, with the rustling of trees or the whispering of soft voices.'.

◄ Dancing on the open-air dance floor at Murray's River Club at Maidenhead, opened by Canadian club owner Jack May in 1915. Illustration by Dorothea St John George in *Nights Out in London*, 1926. (Mary Evans Picture Library)

Skindles outlasted many of its contemporaries, continuing to attract a glamorous, if more eclectic, crowd in the 1950s and '60s – everyone from Mick Jagger to Princess Margaret visited Skindles. But by the 1980s, its status as a local discotheque was something of a humiliating demotion. It was eventually closed in 1995, though in recent years a new Skindles has risen on a different site in Maidenhead, part of the Roux family restaurant empire.

Few of these once-vibrant social spots survived the Second World War and, in fact, many of them began to lose their gloss as well as money in the latter half of the 1930s. Increasing car ownership meant that roadhouses began to attract a more déclassé (i.e. middle-class) crowd and the original early adopters lost interest after the first, few heady years. They were also expensive to run: swimming pools and the West End's finest bands did not come cheap. The war was to sound the final death knell for many, not least because petrol rationing had a direct impact on motoring for leisure. The Lagoon barely lasted six years, closing at the start of the war. The site is now an industrial estate. The Ace of Spades burnt down in the mid 1950s and the area's dubious claim to fame today is as a traffic black spot. The Chase in Ingatestone was demolished to make way for housing estates in the 1960s. A garage now sits on the site once occupied by Murray's in Maidenhead, though its famous lawns survive as a public park. Its neighbour – the magnificent Showboat – became the All Services Club at the beginning of the war before being requisitioned as a factory for Spitfire parts. Post-war, it continued as a factory and never reopened as an entertainment venue, eventually falling into disrepair. At the time of writing, the nautically inspired art deco building, which *The Bystander* in 1933 confidently assured readers would be 'a great success', is set to be demolished to make way for residential flats. ∎